Unforgettable Things

Poems by Sŏ Chŏngju

Translated and with an
Introduction by
David R. McCann

Si-sa-yong-o-sa, Inc.

Published simultaneously in KOREA and the UNITED STATES

Si-sa-yong-o-sa, Inc.
55-1, Chongno 2-ga, Chongno-gu
Seoul 110, Korea

Pace International Research, Inc.
Tide Avenue, Falcon Cove
P.O. Box 51, Arch Cape
Oregon 97102, U.S.A.

ISBN: 0-87296-028-5

This book is a co-publication by Si-sa-yong-o-sa, Inc.
and The International Communication Foundation.

Printed in Korea

Acknowledgments

My thanks, first of all, to the poet Sŏ Chŏngju for his patience, his encouragement, and for the lovely recollection of our first meeting in "David McCann, Translator of my Poems, and the Town of Andong" in this collection.

I am also grateful to Mr. J.S. Min, publisher of this book, for his interest in the project, and especially for the helpful word glosses and other assistance with the translations.

Finally I wish to acknowledge the help of Sandy Lee and Y.H. Kim, both of Cornell University.

Introduction

Sŏ Chŏngju has been an extraordinarily prolific and influential writer. His early "Self Portrait," published in 1938, is a landmark in modern Korean poetry, and with a number of his other poems has become a part of the established canon of twentieth century Korean literary works. His poems have searched into the Silla period, when Buddhism was in official ascendancy (seventh through tenth centuries); through rounds of wandering in and near Korea, and even around the world on a trip in 1977-1978 the poet recorded in the collection "Like the Moon Travelling Westward."

In *Unforgettable Things*, through a series of ninety-two portraits and sketches taken from throughout his life, Sŏ Chŏngju blends portraits of himself into an autobiography that is also a history of Korea, from a distinctive point of view, in the twentieth century. While many of the events alluded to in this collection will be familiar to readers who know Korea even slightly – events such as the Korean War, for example, or the April Revolution that toppled the Syngman Rhee government in 1960 – it may be helpful, nevertheless, to add a few other significant events to the historical background.

*   *   *   *

Sŏ Chŏngju was born in 1915, five years after Japan had established its government-general in Korea and reduced a nation with a long history of independent existence to quasi-colonial status. In 1919, a group of thirty-three Korean patriots, inspired by President Woodrow Wilson's *Fourteen Points* enunciated at the Versailles treaty conference, signed a Proclamation of Korean Independence. The proclamation was read at Pagoda Park in Seoul on March 1. The demonstrations that followed, spreading throughout the country in a matter of days,were brutally suppressed by the Japanese. To the great dismay of the Koreans, who had managed to send a representative to the Versailles conference, Japan turned out to be the only country that took notice of what came to be known as the March First Independence Movement.

The nineteen-twenties and early thirties brought a degree of moderation in the Japanese controls within Korea. With an easing of censorship in the period 1920-1926, especially, the Korean literary world enjoyed a lively renaissance after a decade of near-total silence. New literary groups and their associated journals sprang up like mushrooms; Korean writers tested new ideas about literature and society– and it might be added, did so in a quite lively spirit of collegiality with their Japanese counterparts; and many works by European and American poets and novelists were translated, discussed, modified, adapted as models.

What had been a healthy array of intellectual or artistic differences in the early 'twenties, however, turned rapidly into ideological schism by the end of the decade. Right split from left, and the two were driven further apart by the wedge of Japanese censorship reimposed from 1927 on. Through the nineteen-thirties, the Japanese pursued an increasingly determined effort to break down and eradicate all traces of

Korean national spirit. On February 11, 1940, Koreans were ordered to adopt Japanese names; and the Korean language itself was banned. Severe shortage became a way of life in the nineteen-forties,as food, fuel,as well as any other materials the Japanese identified as necessary for the war effort, were taken from Korea and sent either to Japan or into Manchuria.

Liberation, in 1945, was accompanied by the partition of Korea at the Thirty-Eighth Parallel, a reversion toward the line of demarcation at the thirty-ninth parallel proposed by Russia in 1903 in an attempt to contain the expanding Japanese influence in Korea. Both sides, North and South, struggled for ideological supremacy, the South under Syngman Rhee, installed as president after a three-year period of American military government (headquartered in Japan), and the North under Kim Il Sung.

On June 25, 1950, North Korea attacked the South, starting the Korean War. The fighting ended with the signing, in 1953, of the armistice still in effect today. The mutual hostility of the two governments has not eased.

Syngman Rhee's presidency collapsed on April 19, 1960, when Korean troops refused any longer to beat down the wide-spread demonstrations against election fraud and governmental corruption. A brief democratic interlude ended, in turn, when the coup d'etat of May 16, 1961 installed Major General Park Chung Hee as the military ruler of South Korea.

The economy of Korea enjoyed significant growth under

Park, but his government, like Rhee's before, became increasingly repressive and corrupt. On October 26, 1979, following a series of demonstrations throughout South Korea, Park was assassinated by the head of the Korean C.I.A. Another brief democratic interlude was followed, after nearly a year of intra-military maneuvering and domestic turmoil, by the election on August 27, 1980 of General Chun Doo Hwan as President.

*   *   *   *

The politicization of Korean life discernible from the very earliest part of this collection, reaches its moment of greatest intensity in three poems from the year 1960, one about the close escape of the poet's son from the troops that fired on the student demonstrators on April 19; one about the young high school student who was killed in the demonstrations; and the third, about the poet's arrest, interrogation and evident brush with death at the time of the May 16 coup d'etat. Each occasion might bring to mind a Korean saying: "When whales fight, the shrimp's back breaks." The saying refers to Korea's geopolitical situation, surrounded by and in turn the object of or battleground for the national interests of Japan, China, Russia, and across the Pacific, the United States; but it might also be taken to describe the situation of any individual caught up in the turmoil of Korea's twentieth century. How does one make a life in the midst of it? And beyond that, how does one sustain an artistic life? If it can be done at all, this collection, along with the many other volumes of Sŏ Chŏngju's poetry, shows how.

*   *   *   *

For additional reading on twentieth century Korea, the following books may be of particular interest.

Younghill Kang, *The Grass Roof,* Scribner, 1951. Reissued as a Norton paperback in 1975. A romanticized but evocative portrayal of traditional Korea and the impact of Japan and the West in the early decades of the twentieth century.

Richard E. Kim, *Lost Names, Scenes from a Korean Boyhood,* Praeger, 1970. A boy's life during the period of the Japanese occupation, through the Liberation in 1945.

Chung Chong-wha, ed., *Meetings and Farewells,* University of Queensland Press, 1980. A most intriguing collection of short stories. Not the standard selections, and all the more interesting for that reason.

A selection of fifty-eight poems from Sŏ Chŏngju's earlier books is also available: *Winter Sky,* Poems by Sŏ Chŏngju translated by David R. McCann, in *Quarterly Review of Literature* Contemporary Poetry Series III, Princeton, 1981.

■ CONTENTS

• *Acknowledgements* / **3**
• *Introduction* / **4**

Our Yard / **15**
The Neighborly Persimmon / **16**
Young Watchman / **17**
The Monk Paek Hangmyŏng / **18**
The Concubine's "Drinking Song" / **19**
Recitation / **20**
Grandmother / **21**
First Impression of the Formal Funeral Bier / **22**
The House by the Dragon Spring / **23**
Ten Years Old / **25**
Chrysanthemum and Stone / **26**
Night Road, Moonlight and Frost / **27**
Jealousy / **28**
Parting: a First Lesson / **29**
The Town of Chulp'o (to Young Eyes) / **30**
Saturdays to Grandmother's / **32**
Kŭmsun, the Chinese Noodle House Whore / **33**
Kwangju Student Incident 1 / **35**
Typhoid Fever / **36**
Kwangju Student Incident 2 / **37**
Father's Spoon / **38**
Kwangju Student Incident 3 / **39**
Loss of Virginity / **40**
Refugee? Actor? Or What? / **42**
Frozen Night / **44**

Misa and I and the Carp /45
Ragpicker / 46
Stone Top, the Priest Pak Hanyŏng 1 / 48
With Pak Hanyŏng 2 / 49
The Way to the Diamond Mountains 1 /51
The Way to the Diamond Mountains 2
    From Tanballyŏng Pass to Changansa Temple /54
The Reverend Monk Song Man'gong Amidst
    Peony Flowers / 56
A Declaration of Adulthood / 58
Elected a Poet /60
Miss H /61
Haeinsa Temple   Summer, 1936 /62
Poets Village: Membership and Party /63
Summer on Cheju Island /65
My Marriage / 66
My First Book, *The Flower Snake Collection* / 67
Commemorative for the *Chosŏn Ilbo* Newspaper / 70
On the Naming of My First Son, Sunghae / 72
In Manchuria / 73
On the Playing Field at East Gate Girls High School / 75
Old Man Kkandol from Puldŏmi Village / 76
Return Again when Azaleas are Blooming / 78
Yi Dynasty Porcelain Discovered by Malaria / 80
Atop the Leaning Tower / 83
Liberation / 85
Food and the Anti-Communist Movement / 88
Full-Time Lecturer / 90

The Patriarch Inch'on, the Tonga Daily, and I / **93**
With Dr. Syngman Rhee / **95**
Secretary for Administration / **97**
Autumn, 1949—At the "Flower" Tea Room / **100**
Morning Dive in the Han River—June 28, 1950 / **102**
Potassium Cyanide Left / **104**
Life No Better Than Death / **105**
Suicide Failure / **106**
An Exercise in Harmony / **108**
In Praise of Makkŏlli / **110**
Friends of the Myŏngch'ŏnok in Myŏngdong / **111**
Free Literature Prize from the Asia Foundation of
   America / **113**
Second Fast / **114**
Fainting Spell / **116**
At Sŏrabŏl in Miari / **117**
Doubts at a Doubtless Age / **119**
April 19, 1960 / **121**
April Revolution 2 / **122**
Disaster / **123**
Solution for a Middle-Aged Passion / **126**
Quote: Could I Commit an Act that Heaven would
   Despise? / **127**
Counting Longevity by a Child Late in Life / **129**
Five Years on the Seoul-Ch'unch'ŏn Line / **131**
House of the Apricot Tree / **133**
My Drinking Friend, Pak Kiwŏn / **135**
Story of Ulsan Rock / **137**

Drinking Kimch'i Juice / *138*
Examining a Woman's Fingernails / *139*
As Calamity Begets Good Fortune, Again / *140*
The Power of Sadang-dong and Pongch'ŏn-dong / *142*
The Taiwanese Poet Chung Ting-wen Visits / *144*
Queen Sŏndŏk's Stone / *145*
Chicken Instead of Pheasant / *146*
Forsythia, Ghost in my Garden / *147*
David McCann, Translator of my Poems, and
    the Town of Andong / *149*
Hwan'gap: Full Cycle Sixty Years 1 / *152*
Hwan'gap 2 / *153*
Off on a Trip Round the World / *154*
Doctor of Letters at Sixty, and my Mother / *156*
"Know Grandson" Orchid / *158*
Professor Emeritus / *159*

● *Principal Literary Figures Mentioned in the Poems* / *160*

Unforgettable Things

Our Yard

From spring until fall, in our yard
the smells of wood, all kinds, gathered from the mountain.
Juniper, oak, and prickly ash— the smells
of the rotted wood father gathered to dry for kindling.

At sunset, we spread the straw mat in our yard
and the whole family gathered to eat noodles.
We ate, then lay down and looked at the stars in the sky.
Marveling, we looked at the stars in that marvelous sky.

With the smells of juniper, oak, and ash;
with the smells of our parents' hemp clothes;
with the smell of little brother's pepper,
we stared at those stars as the night sky deepened.

The Neighborly Persimmon

I lived in debt to the persimmon tree
just barely visible across the brook
and over the ramie field at neighbor Chu's house.
There was no persimmon tree at ours.
Even before the sun crossed the ridge,
like a young squirrel, stealing a glance
at the far-away tree, my mouth
starting to water, I dashed through the stream,
soaking my pants to the knees,
and on the way back counted persimmons,
green, that had fallen in the night.
Soaking sour ones in a bowl of water,
I made of each waking hour my time
of persimmons.
                    Even so, our neighbor lady
was a generous soul. When she passed,
carrying the water jar on her head,
she just smiled a faint, half-moon.
She did not let the words
                    "I know what you did"
pass her lips.

Young Watchman

On days when all the family,
mother and grandmother too, went out
to work in the fields, I kept watch,
all alone, over our empty house.
What shall I do if a wolf comes?
What to do if a monk steals
my mother away?
                  In fearful daydreams
I sat at the edge of the porch,
swinging my feet back and forth.
Yet somehow or other, as I rested
my head, my cheek, on the fulling-block stone,
sleep would come.
With the voice of the cuckoo calling from the hill,
held in the cuckoo's call that soaked into the stone
I would fall fast asleep.

The Monk Paek Hangmyŏng

Sŏnun-sa, Zen Cloud Temple, the one place grandmother
would visit each year. On her back,
she would take me when I was five or so,
walking the fifteen *li* of mountain paths
for Buddha's birthday at Sŏnun-sa.
There I saw an old man, grandfather monk
with eyelashes long as a girl's.
His eyes were clear and steady
as my closest friend's, back in the village.
I followed along after that monk
completely at ease.
                    Years later I learned
he was the one that poet-priest Manhae
had sought in his time of despair,
Paek Hangmyŏng, the monk
known as White Crane's Cry.

The Concubine's "Drinking Song"

That part of the season when the ramie was fully grown,
when I was just six I mastered the Book of Ch'u.
Father thought our village teacher had done so well,
he summoned the concubine of Park the tavern master
to perform the Drinking Song and pour the spirits
for our guest.
              Beside them, I was playing
with a bit of bee's wax candle.
The drinking song concubine
had straightened her hair with bee's oil,
and with her silver hair pin,
the red ribbon tied in her hair,
and the gold inlay for her wisdom tooth,
to me this one woman
seemed the most remarkable phenomenon
in the whole world.
            My teacher, my father,
and the Book of Ch'u
seemed quite without substance or meaning.

Recitation

ami sanwŏl kara
ami sanwŏli pallyunch'u hani
yŏngip'pyŏng kang'gangsuryurŭl...

One summer night
beneath the moon
a small crowd of us
seven and eight-year-olds
from the village
school were circling
the mosquito smudge
out in the yard
and reciting in unison
noisy as a flock of baby chicks,
not taken by
the meaning of it,
simply absorbed in the pure
unfathomable sound.
Shouting it out,
mesmerized by the smoke
we sent our voices
out beneath that moon,
with such things
as "the maiden's lovely brow"
never once entering
our heads.

Grandmother

My grandmother worked every day
of every year, in the fields
or in the house.
Without once going
for a visit in the town,
she worked till she wore away
her finger tips.
Village women from time to time
would stop by for a chat.
Her response was
"Chatterbox!"
Nighttimes too,
until the rooster crowed
she would be spinning
her yarn in the corner
of the room by my bed.
Grandmother: she lost
the tips of her little fingers
giving blood for her husband
when he was once deathly ill.
The court dress she brought
in marriage was kept
stored away in a closet,
never worn.
For occasions like Ch'usŏk,
the Autumn Night festival,
Mother would take it out
and just think
What would it be like
to wear this?

First Impression of the Formal Funeral Bier

Not from the sky or the earth but some strange place;
the flower-covered bier had suddenly just appeared
passing our school: "Ŏ-ŏno, Ŏ-ŏno," the dirge.
Seeing it for the first time, fascinated
by this wonder, in a moment when Teacher
had gone out back for a Number Two
I jumped up and ran after the other children,
laughing at the wonder of it, losing
track of everything else.
Teacher whipped our legs when he caught us,
soon after. *Unfair punishment*, I thought
at the time, and I feel the same way now.
Children enjoying such things as that bier
are doing the most natural thing in the world.

The House by Dragon Spring

Where the dragon of the Western Sea
swam fifty *li* through caverns underground,
then rose in the Five Blessings
to ascend into the heavens,
a spring wells up.
Without even a touch of salt,
the waters of that spring tasted
of the Five Blessings.
When I was nine, by great good fortune,
we moved to the mansion by Dragon Spring.

The disposition of the grounds
was so fortunate, the number most numerous
was nine, for the buildings.
For the main gate and the lesser gates,
the number might be large: added up,
they came out of course to eight.
The rooms were arranged in a perfect match
for the Sixty-Four diagram
in the Book of Changes:
With sixty told, just four remained.

The master of that place,
in all the eight provinces
unequalled in wealth,
had gone off to Seoul.
We kept watch
over the empty house.

This affair or not,
my good fortune or another's:
What connection does it have
with being nine years old?
Sliding over the porch floors
was such fun I just went
sliding, never mind
the explanations;
whatever else it was,
a time of sheer joy.

Ten Years Old

The Honorable Mr. Kwak
in the house just behind
had a daughter named Namsuk,
seventeen,
and to me at ten
she was the very best friend,
always happy and kind.
She would pencil the shape
of Chinese pinks,
then ask me to color them in.
I felt sorry each time
I spilled over the lines.
When she asked me to give her
a push on the swing,
I was so happy I broke out in smiles.
Since then, for the swing
or anything else,
with a woman I would rather be
pushing than riding.

Chrysanthemum and Stone

Stone I got, sweaty from the hill climb,
crystal stone put out its white bud.
I planted that stone by the chrysanthemums.

Under the yellow chrysanthemums mother planted and grew,
I set my stone down too, every morning
gave it water to make it grow.

Night Road, Moonlight and Frost

Mother was ill, suddenly, and I had hurried up the valley
to tell my father, some thirty *li* away. Returning
with him, the night made me lonely. In the clear, bright
light of the moon, frost, and soon dawn was near, as I
heard in some distant village the faint crowing of a rooster.
I felt so chilled and lonely, I ducked into the folds
of my father's white cotton coat and walked along holding
tight to the edge of his vest. From time to time I ducked
out again to look and listen for whatever might happen
in the sky and on the earth.

Over a thick field of reeds, a distant flock of wild geese
passed, leaving like the after-tones of dozens of bells
the last *ng* of their *kkirŭrŭng, kkirŭrŭng.* Down
in the gorge below the path we were walking, the river's
waters were brimming over. Father said "Full neap,"
the tide so high that ocean currents had managed to
push their way ten *li* up the river.

In a moment I forgot the cold and loneliness, and began
to feel the composition of all these things was rather
nice after all. Though I did not know the Chinese
characters for composition then, that sense of the
composedness of things I felt that night has come to
be an important standard in my life. What does not
come up to it truly seems rather dull.

Jealousy

Pak Dogong, as they said his name
in their Japanese pronunciation,
was already twenty, clearly the strongest
of all the third graders.
Once when the Japanese
woman teacher had her feet go sore
wearing high heels on a school trip,
he put her on his back
and carried her along.
Just ten at the time,
I felt so jealous of Pak Dogong
my eyes were burning...
How I wished I could
carry her, and jealousy
grew to fill the space
my strength had not yet filled.

Parting: a First Lesson

Miss Yoshimura, our teacher,
when she stood by the flowering radish stalk
her ten half-moons of fingernails
were most extraordinarily beautiful.
In second grade, my class rank
dropped to fifth,
but when this Japanese teacher came
in third grade, she raised
my rank again to first.
Hardly a year passed
before she had to leave.
I bought her long black stockings and a jar
of beauty cream.
As the bus was leaving the village,
our gang squatted down in front
and for quite a time
kept it from going.
She wept, and I cried a lot too
as I learned my first lesson
in parting.

The Town of Chulp'o (to Young Eyes)

Old grandfather selling ginger
I saw at the market every five days.
Long white beard, braided white hair,
and a quick, arresting smile.
Old bachelor grandfather.
Of all Chulp'o's sights,
the ginger root man was my favorite.

Chinese selling hot sweet pancakes;
the ones who sold Shanghai woven socks;
Japanese toffee makers, noodle sellers, bath house keepers
scattered along the wharves,
or on a muddy road beside a ditch:
most of the people of our land
were such a sorry lot
they could not compare with that seller
of ginger root.

Crabs crawling through the reeds,
wild geese flying overhead in the fall,
wild plum blooming by the hedge in spring;
or somehow coming upon a round penny
on a road of mud so deep it swamps your rubber shoes:
such things seemed the most fun of all.

Or if I tired of these, down to the bus barn
I would go, to smell the musty odor

of gasoline. Off to taste that smell
more pungent than garlic.

Spring and autumn, the rattle and the rustle
down by the wharf each day
as sailors and their prostitutes
did their thing. What this
frenzy was, I
had no way of knowing.

When farmhand
             took girl
                         into room,
did it, came
           out, saw
                    me and said
You try it too,
I was
        much too young to try.

Saturdays to Grandmother's

Pines, bamboo,
bean field, bean field,
sesame.
Saturdays, I knew
the smell of sesame.

Sesame smell makes me
remember grandmother.

Past the sesame,
board the ferryboat.
White bearded ferryman with the top knot,
tall and thin as the carved guardian pole.
He rowed me over.
I climbed out at the hill.

Sesame field,
sesame, bean,
then past sesame and bean,
bamboo and pine.
In the pine grove, resin smell
made me long for her
even more.

Kŭmsun, the Chinese Noodle House Whore

When I was twelve, she was
the first girl ever to embrace me.
Smelling of her Ginsuru perfume,
with long braided hair to her thigh,
Kŭmsun, the Chinese noodle shop whore:
What is she doing now?
Where might she be?

Kim Maktong my classmate
twenty years old in fifth grade,
celebrated his marriage by buying a bowl
of noodles for all his friends.
She was the one
brought to sit by our table.
She engaged in that profession
because of food, clothes, sexual
abuse. Syphilis, gonorrhea:
she had often suffered
such diseases. Broken
down by such afflictions,
might she now be lying
white bones in a grave somewhere?

Playing paper, rock, and scissors,
even boys like me seemed to attract her.
Once I took her

into the corner room,
not old enough to know more
rolled around and around with her in my arms
on the floor.

Kŭmsun, O Kŭmsun! Where is our Kŭmsun now?
With her beautiful voice
for the song *Nilliri*,
her eyes so fine, and the gleam
of her teeth so white,
what has become of her now?

Kwangju Student Incident 1

A day in November, 1929,
when the Kwangju student demonstrations
caught fire in Seoul too.
Just thirteen, seventh-grader, I
followed out of curiosity
the upperclassmen who led,
shouting "Long live Korean independence!"
As we reached the headquarters
for the Japanese Governor General, mounted
police drove us like sheep into a corner.
From the police station yard,
one by one we were dragged into a room,
stripped to the waist,
beaten fifteen, twenty times
with leather straps.
Those who had been followers
were turned loose,
though for days after I could not lie down
in bed, for the soreness.
Each day angrier, I muttered at them
"Butcher's bastards! Just you wait!"

Typhoid Fever

It all started in the middle
of spring, my eighth grade year
when I had turned fourteen.
I don't know why, but everything suddenly
seemed unbearably pitiful.
I decided to change
from a first to a third class room,
in the slum.
Threw my new shoes away
and started going around in those Chiggadabi's
the laborers wore.
Eating cheap and unclean food
I wound up finally with a case of typhoid
so severe I couldn't sweat.
In my impoverished hermitage
far from the village,
I was abandoned by my father.
Only Mother stayed by me, praying
"Take me instead of him. Take me!"
With a fever above forty degrees,
I became a fantastic bird,
flying like Peter Pan, wandering
over many seas and mountains.
Over a vast wilderness of uncertain
disgust, I practiced and practiced
how to fly.

Kwangju Student Incident 2

After typhoid, my hair
all fell out. Back in school
second term, the only thing
that seemed any fun to do
was climbing the hill behind the school
at recess to eat the piece of cake or bread
I bought.

When this one fellow who had the nickname
Gandhi came up and said "How about
stirring up another incident like the last?"
it seemed like just a fine idea.
I became one of the leaders.

And when, dressed in the blue clothes
of a prisoner, I approached
Miura, the public prosecutor,
he said "So, you miss your mother, don't you?"
I burst into tears, forgetting

my pride quite completely.
Released, indictment suspended,
I fell short once again
of being honored for
distinguished service.

Father's Spoon

At his evening meal, Father
saw me and dropped his spoon.
It clattered and jangled.
As a leader of the second Kwangju students affair,
I had been thrown out of school into jail.
Turned loose, I went home
and performed my bows to him,
and the spoon, my father's , just fell
from his hand.
I earned thereby another
mark of distinction—
Unfilial Son—for keeping
my father from eating his meal.

Kwangju Student Incident   3

Spring of 1931, I transferred
to the Chŏnbuk Comprehensive High School.
Over and over, I would hear "Oh,
you're Sŏ Chŏngju, the one expelled from Central?
I'm So-and-So, expelled from Such-and-Such.
Let's try it again here."

They were a bother, but I could not avoid
my duty all alone, so once again I became
a suspicious character, organizing
alliances, gathering secret unions.

When the principal called us in, at last,
he said "The police are insisting we dismiss you.
If that happens, you won't be able to enter
another school. Let me advise you, therefore,
to withdraw, on your own initiative."

As I consider his sincere and gentle request,
it occurs to me that he had some understanding
of our lot.

Loss of Virginity

On days when the snow fell in huge petals
I feared the herdsman with whiskers on his chin,
the one who went down the road with his herd
of a dozen bulls, or so.
I shall explain why.

One snowy winter day when I was sixteen,
expelled from the village, I wandered
aimlessly along the new road
till I saw a small shop, the kind you set up
in a corner of the house.
"Do you have any *makkŏlli?*" I asked,
stepping in.

        "It's so cold out today, young man.
Why don't you come into the room?"
A pleasant-looking woman of about thirty
asked me in.

I warmed my hands over the straws burning
in a sheet-metal stove,
and drank nearly two kettles full,
filling the glass, drinking a toast,
until suddenly the woman
grabbed me. In a moment I held her,
we toppled over, and like a stroke
of lightning it was done.

I learned the husband
was the herdsman, well known
as a fearsome fellow,
so if for some reason I had to pass the place,
I went the long way round,
out by the embankment and over the paddy paths.
And whenever it snowed like that,
I worried about that herdsman
with the bushy beard.

Later still, I discovered
the fearful herdsman with all the hair
was unable to have any children.
He had taken three wives,
but still had no descendants
even at fifty.

He told his second and third wives
"Listen, woman. Even a wanderer on the road,
grab him and see if you can't
give us a child."
Earnestly, they said, and sincerely,
he had asked.

When I had learned all about it,
the whole situation seemed so amusing
that even big petals of snow
were enough to make me laugh.

Refugee? Actor? Or What?

Thrown out of school twice,
I could not face my parents.
I went in and out extremely
carefully, watching their faces
for some sign of their intentions.
Thinking of running off to Shanghai
to join the Independence Party,
I took three hundred *wŏn*
from my father's desk.
I was in Seoul, ready to leave
when quite by accident
I found myself listening
to some *kayagŭm* player
who sang "Listen to me, Oh traveller;
Listen to the story I have to tell."
Just because I happened to hear it,
instead of buying a revolver
for my work in Shanghai, I bought
one suit and fancy tie,
turning my sights to an apprenticeship
with the Academy of the Arts.
I played one of the minor characters
in an amusing play, "The Prosecutor,"
by Gogol,
but that too failed, in the end,
to suit me.

I went off to the National Library
and started reading such things
as Turgenev's romantic stories.
Just hanging about like that
became my favorite occupation.
In order to specialize
in such thoroughgoing lassitude,
I went so far as to seek out
a Buddhist retreat, deep in the mountains,
where I spent the entire winter.

     kayagǔm: A zither-like stringed instrument.

Frozen Night

I knew
one winter's night at seventeen
how those who freeze to death
die.
Frozen night,
midnight, twenty Centigrade
below, and I was running
across Water Mark Bridge
over Ch'ŏng'gyech'ŏn,
calling to the beggar family
in the tent below
"Hello! Hello! Hello! Please,
just tonight let me have a place
to sleep."
          No matter
how I called and called,
it was no use. Only "Hey, you!
There's not enough room for us
in here!"

With this answer echoing around me
in the freezing air,
and without another idea
where to try,
I came to know what they call
the fatal moment for one
who freezes to death
from the inside.

Misa and I and the Carp

When being a refugee, a tragic figure,
or the son of a rich landlord didn't work out,
I read Turgenev.
When nervous breakdowns or the *kayagŭm*
lost their charms, Misa would bend
and sharpen a bit of wire for a fishing pole.

Spring nights, when cherry blossoms were at their best
in Ch'anggyŏng Park, hundreds of people would go to see.
Misa and I would sneak in with the crowd
and fish for carp from the pond edge
by the pavilion.

Misa brought a sack tied to his waist under his jacket,
a sack for the carp we caught.
Sprinkling custard cake in the space beneath the pine tree,
hidden from sight he fished like a python,
like the flying tiger.

Standing a short distance away,
able to hide him behind me,
I whistled a tuneless song,
keeping a most fluent watch.
The *thrill* of it was unsurpassed,
and the taste of the carp we caught and ate
was worth anything you could possibly give.

Ragpicker

In the fall of my seventeenth year
I became a ragpicker.
Carrying a heavy bag on my back
I searched through the trash cans of Seoul.
Knowing this might be the last thing I could do,
I searched all the alleyways, all the corners.

When I got no more than twenty *chŏn*
for all I picked in a day to sell,
I spent five for radish leaf stew
in the morning, five for a pancake at lunch,
and ten for the cheapest dinner to be found.

I once lay resting on the lawn behind the British legation
when a foreign girl, fresh and pretty as a rose,
passed by. She turned her face
with a show of such deliberate disdain,
I burned at the shame of it...

When once from a trash can at some Japanese house
I retrieved an old *Yudambu* bed warmer,
I gave it to Pombu, my friend's oldest brother.
Pombu made a poem about it:
"...leaning on a trash can, exhausted
voice of the *p'iri* reaches out,
exquisite turnings..."
Such a phrase was to be found as well,
stuffed down into it all.

Yudambu: The brand name, evidently, according to the author's note.
p'iri: A reed instrument having a piercing, nasal tone.

Stone Top, the Priest Pak Hanyŏng   1

Because I had actually been a ragpicker,
with a smile like a peony
he greeted me as if I were some spirit friend
from heaven—the priest Pak Hanyŏng
seemed like a classmate
from primary school.
"So you really went and did that sort of thing?
Good bone for the way! Bone for the way.
It's good you did that,
and now that you have, stay
here now and study with me.
Hee hee hee hee hee! It's good
you have come! Welcome indeed!"
He held my hand tight as he spoke,
did Pak Hanyŏng, the priest.
There could be no more than one
laugh like his, soaring like the laugh
of the morning skylark;
following, I stayed by his side
for a time.

With Pak Hanyŏng 2

Spring of 1934.
In the azalea air
behind the temple
I was smoking a cigarette
in the yard when someone
in a voice that made my ears ring
bellowed "Hey, Chŏngju! You look
like a chimney!
Don't you feel ashamed,
on a clear day like this?
Ch'oe Namsŏn smoked
until he was thirty-three,
but he gave it up for his studies.
Go on like that, at your age,
and what will you make of yourself at all?"
When I turned,
it was Master Stone Top.
More the strong tone of concern
in his voice
than the meaning of what he said:
quite without my willing it
I dropped the cigarette.

I was summoned to his room
a few days after.
"You don't seem
the kind of person
to be a monk.

More an Yi Paek
or So Tongp'a, the kind
who fly about like storks
or such, and somehow
try to live by writing.
Don't be just like them, though.
Prepare for a place
like our Buddhist seminary.
Study the philosophers and poets,
and then be a poet.
For you, that's best."

So he told me, and again I made ready
to go off to school, thanks to which
following Liberation I became a teacher
at Tongguk University, wrote
poems for a living and did not starve.

The Way to the Diamond Mountains   1

When I said to Priest Stone Top
"I think I'll go to the Diamond Mountains
and practice meditation," he looked
clear within me, laughed
and replied "So, you're going
to do some sightseeing? Well, come back
when you are ready."
He reached over to me
the pair of old, comfortable shoes
he always wore.
That way ran a path
through the entire universe.
Glancing away for just a moment,
he said "Walking will be best,"
and laughed once again.

By the lunar calendar
it was the third or fourth of May,
I suppose. In my white cloak
of ramie cloth,
and with an old straw hat
perched on my head,
I was so excited at going,
even more than the destination,
I rushed off to the Diamond Mountains
swift as a river current.

I stopped at Mangwŏl Temple
in Yangju, the first night.
The delay for eating and sleeping
at first seemed unbearable,
but at night when I saw stars far larger,
brighter, more numerous
by far than Seoul, I came to know
for the first time the fresh taste
of truly counting them.

Next day to Simwŏn Temple,
all the way to Yongch'ŏn.
There they wrapped up
some of the rice cakes
left over from services.
I was on my way to Top'i-an Temple
in Ch'ŏlwŏn, carrying that package
and just listening to the cuckoos calling
when a girl with the most lovely eyes
who had been washing clothes in a mountain stream
looked at me and smiled.
Like the moon in the day.
Even approaching seventy now,
I cannot forget her
                    truly
most precious gift.

Walking on for the fourth day
I flew like a sparrow into Ch'ŏnbul Temple
in Kŭmsŏng.
Suspicion

of the outside world
lingered there.
They considered me and said
memorize the Thousand Hands Invocation.
I suppose they intended to learn
if I was worth the bed and board.
After I passed, they treated me
to millet, and I learned
only then
the special taste it possesses.

Ah, how splendid! How truly extraordinary!
The good priest Stone Top
knew of all these flavors well before.
He made me walk
so I would taste each one.
Truly, how remarkable
he was!

The Way to the Diamond Mountains   2

From Tanballyŏng Pass to Changansa Temple

From Seoul I walked five days to Tanballyŏng
thinking of Mawi who crossed
at the fall of the kingdom of Silla.
Toward sunset, I was making my way
slowly toward Ch'angdo Village.
As one fellow with a bitter smile
approached, I asked "Please,
could I stay just the one night
at your home?"
                    Gently,
he refused, saying
                    "Ours
is only one room."
The exquisite taste of fifty
or sixty *li* travel by night
from Tanballyŏng straight on to Changansa
was thereby given me.
Not without the smell of tigers, either,
on a fearful, painful, hungry way...
The taste at the end of that dead-end alley
I had to go panting over:
That taste too, I was given to try.

Resentment and despair
may well be more exhausting
than the struggle against lost time,
but the truly bitter taste,
if bitterness is true of it,
of "No home for the son of man":
—I came to know the flavor
more strongly than before.

The Reverend Monk Song Man'gong
Amidst Peony Flowers

Crossing over Myŏnggyŏngdae from Masayŏn,
a field
    like heaven's gate—
red peonies in full bloom.
Rising over that field in cold
desolation, a house with a black-tiled roof.
Entering that house, the main room,
on every side, nymphs' smiles,
and Man'gong seated in the most comfortable spot
like the greatest hero of all time.

With the air of one
who might have been MacArthur's older brother,
and with cheeks shining with the color of peaches,
he simply sat there, in the midst
of all the smiles of those flower-like
ladies, saying "Oh, is that so?
Ah, is that so?"
In some agitation, I raised my voice
and shouted out "Venerable priest, I want
to practice Zen under your guidance."
He replied "Don't hurry so.
Go outside, for a start, and relax.
You've come all the way to the Diamond Mountains,
so have a look around."
And with that, he went

to great pains to ignore me,
returning to his "Ah,
is that so?" and again
"Ah, is that so?"
and again.

At this my patience broke.
I went up to Pirobong Peak,
round to Kuryongyŏn Waterfall,
and then with a visit here and there by Haegŭmgang,
took the train at Changjŏn
and went back to Seoul.

A Declaration of Adulthood

A student in class lost his watch.
"Who took it?" the students said,
looking at this one's expression,
and that one's. Bearing it all in silence
might have been better, but seeing
those questioning eyes directed at me
I could not stand it, feeling
heat rising inside.
              "All right,
outside!" I said, dragging
that man of power who lost his watch.
At the top of my voice I shouted
"You fool! You made the mistake!
You lost the watch! You lost it!
So stop acting suspicious of the rest of us!"
Out there in the sunlight
I bellowed at him.

There were some students since then
who said "A strange fellow.
If he didn't steal it,
that should be enough. Why does he make
such a spectacle of himself?"
They took to watching me
with the kind of suspicion in their eyes
that runs on forever.

However that may be,
this one declaration at the time
was my first public statement
since I had begun wearing
the student's four-cornered hat,
the year I became an adult.

Elected a Poet

In the fall of 1935 I wrote a poem in some depression,
a poem called "The Wall," and sent it to the reader's column
at the Tonga Daily.
                    Come winter, it still had not been
published, so I gave it up, thinking "Another rejection."
On a day in December, a registered letter arrived
from the Daily. Opening it, I learned
"The Wall" had been chosen for the New Spring Literature
Prize.
    Probably tossed on someone's desk in the literature
department and left unread until somehow it was mixed in
with the entries for the competition.
                                    More likely
there just weren't any strong entries that year,
so mine emerged entirely by good luck.
Live long enough, and there are such fortunate occasions.

Miss H

At the crossroads where willows hang their branches
a pretty fox magically changing
Ah-ah! popping out
mirage? Musk
pouches on her back?
Strip of silk on the shrine
of some local deity?
Since the time I awoke
from that sleep,
I had been wandering about
kept away by the winds blowing
until several moons had waned
standing, crying like a telephone pole
Again
all the heels of my socks
became nothing but holes
while I wandered in this temple yard
And so.
I mean the start
of my being set free,
when she no longer could bear
the smell of my feet in those holey socks
and quietly turned her attention toward
that man not getting
holes in his socks.

Haeinsa Temple

Summer, 1936

Drinking four or five pots of *makkŏlli*
and eating bits of dried pollock with the fat
laughing old woman who kept the wine shop,
or entering the clear stream in the valley
and then dozing for a while...
The *kkirŭrŭk* sound as the pheasant
flew from the barley field,
I could sense even down to my toes.
Beside a peony bed in the barley field
a young bachelor farmhand stood,
blushing to the tips of his ears;
taking along the young mistress,
blushing as he stood there,
while I secretly enjoyed the scene,
feeling slightly envious,
then returning to my room
and fastening the door shut,
performed the shameful
shameful rite of X.

At night I would open every window
to the owl's night sky,
then catch the miserable bats that came swarming in
and nail them to the wall, crucifying them,
and after the sun came up,
go down to the primary school
at the temple and teach
the children.

Poets Village: Membership and Party

Putting in his pocket
the last will and testament
of his father who had died in prison,
Ham Hyŏngsu went out in the bright moonlight
through Sŏngbuk-dong, playing a serenade
on his harmonica.

On Kugang Mountain, the arrowroot vines
 have wrapped themselves round Green Stone Rock.
The water from the spring by that rock was so sweet,
 I cried without holding back.
The one who has gone, the one who has gone,
 has never been back here again.
Kim Tongni simply hid in the mountains,
sent verses like this, but never came out.

Chosen for a nicely ripened widow's lot,
O Changhwan would appear with his nose bleeding.
I was giving him lessons in drinking
the strong, Chinese *ppaegal.*

Yi Yonghŭi, eldest son of Mr. Yi Kapsŏng,
sported his grandfather's straw lid of a hat.
As a college student, always dressed in Korean costume,
he did rather well at Latin and Greek and gambling too.

Yi Sŏngbŏm, private tutor at the residence
of the emperor's in-laws,

had the best income among us.
From time to time he bought us drinks
at a Chinese restaurant in Sŏsomun.
For drinks, that strong but cheap *ppaegal*, of course,
and for eats, something we called *boil-dagen.*
We collected the left-overs,
what the others didn't eat,
scraped them all together
and warmed the mess up.
That's why we called it
boil-dagen.

Summer on Cheju Island

Above Chŏngbang Waterfall in Sogwip'o on Cheju,
that barley field in the clear, hard sunlight,
and the song of the lark in the sky above that field!
I who had come this far was no longer human,
but just a small and weary spirit lying on its back
on a path through a field
with my belly button showing.

The only thing that entered my mouth was the burning *soju*
  --that, and seaweed soup with *pomal* mussels.
I threw up rice, barley, everything else.
With a cry like a rooster's at the dawn of creation,
kko-kkiyo, kko-kkiyo, my insides cried out.

Already in such an alcohol-ridden and sex-less state,
I could only be a genuinely sorry fool
for the diving women who approached me, dancing.
If a pretty girl had come to me,
there in the old pine grove where the stars
were all shining like candles,
and if she had settled down beside me, saying
"Why don't we see about trying an engagement,"
I could have managed only my feeble grin,
like the hawk that missed the pheasant.

> *Pomal* mussels: shellfish, at any rate.
> The shells are thrown in playing *yut,* the
> New Year's board game. *Pomal* is Che-
> ju dialect, though the author does not
> know the meaning.

My Marriage

"She was cleaning vegetables for *kimch'i*
there by the well. When I looked out
from the men's quarters, through the gaps
in the twig fence the sight of her
bending forward so purposefully as she worked
was enough. 'We'll do it,' I thought,
and went right ahead with the marriage agreement.
So don't let me hear another word;
just prepare yourself for your wedding."

That is how Father selected my bride-to-be.
To check whether the choice was the right one,
I dealt out the *hwat'u* cards to see.
The four of empty mountain came out right,
as did the four of red clover.
The moon on empty mountain was my love,
while the red bush clover was the procurator.
The sign was very clear:
I should take the girl to wed.
The four chrysanthemums were the wine,
while the four in autumn leaves were my worries.
They did appear all at once,
but that kind of thing is part of it too...

On my wedding day, at any rate,
as I pondered these matters seated up on a donkey's back,
how it had turned out seemed in the end
more advanced than the scientific
or love affair route toward a marriage.

My First Book, *The Flower Snake Collection*

The first edition
of my very first
collection, *Flower Snake,*
published in the winter
of 1938 was truly a leper's
bit of boasting.
In its entirety, it came
to less than fifty
pages, but one in a special binding
was priced at five *wŏn*
with the regular one going
for three.
Never in the entire history
of our country's publications
has there ever been a book
more expensive,
while even at that the print run
came to just one hundred and thirty.

The cover
of the special edition
was painter's canvas,
while the back was pure silk.
The blood-red title was done
in embroidery.
The pages were hand-laid paper from Chŏnju,

each several sheets rolled together,
then beaten smooth.

Some time after
placing them in Yi Ponggu's book shop,
I heard that one
had been purchased
by a moderately well-to-do
kisaeng.
O, how absolutely truly glorious!
With the payment for that one
book, I went round and round
all the bars and drank
a hundred rounds or more
with anybody at all.

Kim Kirim, Im Hwa, Kim Kwanggyun and O Changhwan
must have had the same leper's
madness as I, back then.
Each one emptied his wallet,
putting ten *wŏn* into the pool
for a publication party for nine
at the Bright Moon Garden restaurant.

That is what I saw
written in their faces
as they came to celebrate
this display of pride.
At such moments, trouble
can easily follow,

but I stayed somehow within myself,
feeling in some way at fault.

That sense of shame I learned
growing up beneath our village sky
was the reason I maintained
self control.

Commemorative for the
Chosŏn Ilbo Newspaper

Whatever I am doing, it is my nature
often to have my mind on other things
with my two eyes following,
so even during the turbulent summer of 1940
I went off in a friend's fishing boat.
I roamed around on the Western Sea,
reading old classics like The Flower in the Prison.
Returning home, I found
a notice had come from the *Chosŏn Ilbo*
requesting a commemorative poem.
There was a letter too,
from the poet Kim Kirim,
the cultural affairs editor,
and even a telegram reminder.
August the tenth, the day of publication,
was well past, and with it, the chance to write
and leave something behind.

I wrote it, nevertheless.
Though I had nowhere to send it, I wrote
> *Party ended./ Seated for the last time*
> *we eat rice soup,/ start a red fire,/ leave*
> *the ashes behind./ Twilight, as we fold*
> *the tents./ Standing, we thank our host.*
> *At the end feeling a bit drunk,/ all of us*
> *now returning.*

O my neck! my neck! my neck! my neck!
From the distant sea,/ the beating sound
of my bell, plunging.

Writing almost in tears, I set it down,
this much, at least, not done
with my attention wandering.

On the Naming of
My First Son, Sunghae

In the purely traditional way, my wife
gave birth to our first child without a doctor.
In the middle of the night as she lay sweating
I had gone to fetch some clear well water,
and holding it in the gourd dipper, I prayed.
This way, the shaman had told me,
the birthing will come easier.

When our little one turned out
to have arrived with a pepper attached,
I gave him the boy's name Sunghae,
the very first thing that had come into my head.
It means *drawing sea water in a gourd.*

Long, long ago there was a foolish man
who had dropped a pearl into the ocean.
To get it back, he would dip
sea water in a gourd.
For my son as well, no other approach
could be superior to that.
For him to wait patiently drawing the sea:
that was the half-baked idea behind
naming my son *Sunghae.*

In Manchuria

For the rice to live on with my wife and child
I took a job at the Kando branch
of the Manchu Grain Company.
The head of the place was a Japanese,
a former chief of patrolmen,
and from the start he spoke to me
in the lowest forms of address.
  "Hey, Cho! You
    take those Chinese brats outside
    and you get those stamps onto the timbers
    out there in the yard."
That low-life put on airs in the most boorish manner.

The Chinese kids were going "Teacha, Teacha, it's cold"
in winter weather running thirty below
while I threw the hammer for those metal plates
over my shoulder and back down with a steady
Bang Bang Bang,
working into a mountain of logs.
The sky broke into great lumps of pain,
my palms were worn raw;
the whole business was infuriating.

At night, back at the boarding house
I lay with the quilt pulled over my face,
wondering how to tweak that bastard's nose.
One after the other I dug out and considered

all the cases of revenge I knew of, East or West.
I compared them all, till well after midnight.

Next day, I went straight from work
to the Turkish furrier's
and bought a leopard waistcoat
on the installment plan.
I had my hair carefully trimmed
at the barber's, then took my three-piece
wedding suit out to be cleaned and pressed.

At last came the morning of the day
when all my preparations were complete.
Looking far more imposing than the chief,
I went in, sat down in the office, and watched
the bastard for his reaction.

No disappointment. I had him just where I wanted.
For the first day or two, he kept an uneasy silence.
Then "Hey, Sŏ!' was changed to "Mr. Sŏ,..."
He finally started using the polite forms.
As I sat there in my three-piece
with the leopard waistcoat,
looking, I imagine, like his own boss
back in the main company office,
he began to wonder just what kind of connections
this Mr. Sŏ possessed, just how high and deep
they ran. He began to feel a bit nervous.
He began to feel it, and that precisely
was the mark I had been aiming for.

On the Playing Field at East Gate Girls High School

In the summer of 1941
I had only my one suit,
winter weight, so when I taught
gym at East Gate Girls High,
I wound up wearing my Korean clothes
of white ramie-cloth.
I would be raising my two arms,
lowering them,
stretching out,
then closing up
while I kept the count in Japanese
ichi-ni, ichi-ni.
I looked like a crab trying
to hide its eyes.
Ch'oe Chŏnghŭi, the novelist,
looked in as she was passing by
and said it was truly
quite a sight.

Old Man Kkandol from Puldŏmi Village

Mr. Kkandol from Puldŏmi
was so poor his crap-hole had run dry.
He had no patience,
took someone's ox during the night,
and after a few years in jail,
came back to discover his wife had gone off
and had a baby with someone else.
When he found her, snuffling away
wherever it was she hid,
he said to her "Come on. It's all right."
He just brought her back, never
saying anything to blame her at all.

Somehow he seemed to know the nature
of young Chŏngju quite thoroughly,
and he put together a deed that said
he had sold the few acres
— though really he hadn't —
of land that my father had left me.

When the false deed was exposed,
for his part in forging the seal
and such matters, he was bound to go
back into prison again;
but considering the principal
still would remain, despite the loss,
and besides, that his teeth, still hard and white

looked good, I just had the whole business
quietly set aside.

At this, what a glad invitation he extended
to visit his home in Puldŏmi.
"Chŏngju, listen. Hey?
It would really be nice
if you and I could go fishing.
Hey? Hee hee hee..."

So I went with him, and we cast the net,
laughing together in great bursts,
and his laughter was far brighter
than mine.
And although he was sixty, when I happened to see
that thing, his seemed
far more strongly formed than mine.

As we drank together and ate the raw fish,
he spoke to me
          "Hey, no-good!
That was a crazy thing to do,
what you did. A crazy thing to do!"
As he might have teased his own
young lover.
          How good it would be,
if the heavens allowed,
to name him the real honor student.

Return Again when Azaleas are Blooming

A shameful thing,
when I think of my father's passing,
but I sold the land I inherited,
filled my pockets to bursting,
and flourishing wads of ten-thousand *wŏn* notes,
swaggered around in the world.
I simply used it all up,
and what a business that was,
just using it up!
Growing damp in the early autumn rains
I trudged along some sea-side road,
and if I spied a jar
of some little tavern's flower wine,
I knew I had found paradise itself.
With the quick and pungent smell
of flower wine, and seated at the warm spot
in a nicely comfortable room
with a pleasant lady who sang
our lively folksongs nicely,
and with a plump, moist hen
all cooked to a turn—
filling the glasses,
exchanging the toasts
through one full jar of wine
I drank it all down.

Whether the folksong-singing wine lady
was older than me or not,
and whether she happened to be another's wife,
turning fresher with each drink
I would give her little baby kisses,
and she
　　"Come back again, come again when the azaleas
are blooming."
　　　　　　And I,
　　　　　　　　　"What are you saying?
Of course I'll be back, of course I will."

Though all of this was nothing but lighthearted chatter,
still I find it worth having as a keepsake.

Yi Dynasty Porcelain Discovered by Malaria

When the Pan-Asian War broke out,
stirred up by the Japanese,
every bit of food was taken
for the soldiers. In Seoul,
even barley and wheat
were drained down to the bottom.
A teacher's salary each month
wouldn't buy two *mal* of black market rice.
Old man Pyŏn Suju and I
stood with all the other drinkers
in the long, thin line
that stretched from the corn-mash *makkŏlli*
rationing place, down the first block of Chongno,
all the way out to East Gate.
Our turn never came,
even for a single bowl.

My wife couldn't stand the hunger,
so she took our child and set off
on a begging trip,
back to her home in Chŏlla province.

I roasted up a handful
of left-over barley, ate it
and lay down.
Thanks to the noisome mosquitoes,

I was stricken with malaria.
After two or three attacks,
my conscious soul left me
and I flew like Peter Pan
far above this land of three-thousand *li*.

Following the fifth attack,
wearing nothing but my ramie coat
I climbed on the trolley from Noryangjin
to East Gate. Once moving, I remembered
I had no destination,
so I climbed off again at the third block
of Chongno, and boarded the trolley
for Noryangjin.

As the trolley passed the market at South Gate,
opposite my window, in an antique shop display
the color of the Yi dynasty white porcelain bowl
is something I shall never forget.

It swept over me like a tidal wave,
or the very voice of heaven,
or the dead souls of our forefathers
joined again in unison.

"I am going, I am going, I am going away.
Do I have the money for the journey toward death?"
I sang to myself this quick little song,
while the white, so white to almost blue
left me no hiding place, no way to turn:

color without recompense, eternal and absolute.
Color that survived purely within itself.

Acquainted with that color for the first time,
and confiding in it openly, I joined at last
in the quiet respiration of the old ones
who long ago had lived unseen by any others.

Atop the Leaning Tower

It was in 1944, when azaleas were about to bloom.
Lying asleep one chilly morning near dawn,
I woke in terror from a dream of being at the top
of the Leaning Tower of Pisa as it eased
farther and farther over until I was certain
I was about to die. There was a sudden Bang.
When I opened the door to the next room,
the wall clock had fallen to the floor,
and soon after, the policeman Kim Sanggil,
a detective from the secret police
in Koch'ang, near my home town,
came bursting into my rooms
and snapped handcuffs around my wrists.

Though I had no idea what it was about,
I went off with him, to be locked up
at the Koch'ang police station.
"Listen, you lowlife! What's all this
about you gulping down *soju*
every day at sundown in the market place
and whining about how you can't stand it any more?
You're so depressed you can't
stand it any more?
        Well now a bunch
that call themselves your followers
have put together a theatre group
and they're going around from village to village.
Do you know the play they're doing,
you miserable wretch? Do you?"

So that was the reason he had come for me.
I spent three months and ten days inside,
where the only pleasures were catching
the lice that crawled through my shirt,
and sharing a bit of porgy stew
with my neighbor cell-mate, Kim Pangsu,
when they could bring it from his home.

Another cell-mate's son had been drafted
as a laborer in Hokkaido.
He slept with the son's wife
who hatched a baby he then killed.
When that felon was brought in, he started
singing the Fisherman's Song,
and I chimed right in.

When they took him off to the prosecutor's,
that guy handed me two or three thousand *wŏn*
without letting the guard see.
I didn't even throw it away,
but stuffed it down in my shirt.

The police captain who came from headquarters
to look into my own case
was a Japanese I had gotten to know
when I was home from college one time.
He was the one
I had read the poet Ishikawa Takuboku with,
and mindful of that, he effected
my release.
            Turned loose like that,
still I proceeded; I did come out.

Liberation

All of our countrymen were saying
I will become president,
or vice president at least,
but first let's fill
our empty stomachs
from the bottom to the top.
Plough oxen were slaughtered
at random and turned
into meat.
The rice disappeared
from the fields and was made
into *ttŏk* cakes to eat
or *yakju, soju,* and *makkŏli* to drink.
Then with just about everything
eaten and drunk,
pandamonium.
Every single railroad car
bound for Seoul
had all its windows smashed.
Even the locomotive
rooftops were jammed with riders.
Left divided from right
and the factions began fighting.
The clever ones thought
to get their share from all this
and started up their businesses,
while the ones who considered
themselves more refined

kept watch at a distance,
thinking it would all work out
somehow.

My friend Mongni opened
a wine house in Chongno.
Pyŏn Suju and Kwŏn Aeyu
often went there.
Together, we worked
at easing our hunger,
waiting to see
how the situation
might develop.

Somewhat
later, I realized
Kwŏn Aeyu must have cast
his lot and seen
the appearance of all things
working out
was false,
for he simply
disappeared
from this earth.
It was not suicide,
homicide, death
from an illness.
Like the poet Li Po
who fell into the water
and went up to heaven,
without a ripple

he was gone.
Li Po accomplished it
at the height of excitement,
but Aeyu's brow
had shown nothing
but worries.

By what means could he
have gone like that?
Even at his own house,
no one in his family knew
where he went,
how he disappeared.

Note: It is said that the Chinese
poet Li Po, seeing the moon in the
water and thinking to embrace it,
fell out of a boat and drowned.

Food and the
Anti-Communist Movement

In the winter of 1945
following Liberation, the way
the communists took advantage
of the American military government's policy
of equal recognition
seemed detestable.
I joined the Anti-Communist Youths
Association, and rode around
in the back of a truck
going "Destroy the communists! Destroy them!"
Chang Chunha, Son Kijŏng and others
all joined in with a will.

For a time it went along splendidly,
but then what kind of low business was it?
Doesn't one have to get something
to eat?

After careful thought and deliberation
I came up with my own subsistence plan.
I am ashamed to describe it, but in outline
it went approximately as follows.

In bookshops beyond West Gate
I could buy cheap
the books left behind by the Japanese.

With a rubber eraser I would carefully expunge
the price written in the back,
then carry them down to the bookstores
in Insadong or Ch'ungmuro,
and realize a small profit on the transaction.
I did it whenever I had the time,
knowing full well, I confess,
it was hardly the decent and proper thing to do.

Full-Time Lecturer

November of 1946.
To find again some way
to eat and live,
I put the bed quilts
over my shoulder
and threw in my lot
with the crowd on the train
to Pusan.
I had been offered
a lectureship
at the newly opened
Tonga University.

Though I looked like a good-for-nothing,
I well remembered how university professors
had carried themselves
during the Japanese time,
so I put on a white vest,
second-hand,
and a necktie
that seemed dignified,
and arrived for classroom duty
inside some warehouse the Japanese Empire
had left behind
in Tongdaesin-dong.
My style must have seemed about right,
even to those students just back
from studies in Japan,

for they all called out "Hey, that's great!"
and gave me a round of applause.

The problem, though,
was what to lecture on,
what to teach and win their interest
so I could eat.
Those who were known
as our college students, those days,
were unable to take proper notes
in our language.
When I introduced the method
and held them to it,
they couldn't manage to be other
than obedient.

Teaching this way
by turns to the whole student body,
getting into the spirit
of eight hours of talking
every day, at night
when I went back to my unheated
upper-story room,
my legs quivered and shook.

Sea-squirt and clam stew
were the things to eat in Pusan,
but the strong rice wine
was best of all.
It would have been hard to live
without it.

On days with no classes
I went out with Yi Pongnae
a Fisheries College student.
Wandering about, shoulder to shoulder
we drank as if we were majoring in it.

One other noteworthy
element in my life
was the little shack of a trailer
pulled by a pony.
I didn't have a penny to send home to Seoul,
but going off to teach
with the jangling pony bell,
my spirits were not so bad, after all,
as I closed my eyes gently
and let my mind wander.

The Patriarch Inch'on,
the Tonga Daily, and I

Summer of 1931,
Mr. Kim Sŏngsu, known as Inch'on,
returned home, and since I
came from the same county,
I went to pay my respects.
When asked which bus I had taken,
I answered in hasty confusion
"By the fourth O'clock."
"Well, four O'clock is four O'clock,
and the fourth hour will be the fourth hour,
but tell me, does our language
possess a fourth O'clock too?
Really now, young man!"
Upon returning home
quite thoroughly ashamed,
I decided to put all my energy
into mastering our language,
and on January first, 1936,
my poem "The Wall" was awarded first prize
in the Tonga Daily's
spring literature competition.

Afterwards, in 1945,
following Liberation
and during the time of the American military government,
I was chosen as city editor for the Daily,
and was treated to lunch

at the same table with Inch'on.
He said "So, you've turned out
to be quite a poet,
quite versed in our language?
Well done;
that's well done.
Now then, do your best
to improve our Tonga Daily as well."
He gave me that encouragement
and praise as if the "Fourth O'clock" incident
had taken place only the day before.

Accordingly, I adopted
something like the following
as my literary attitude and program:
"Even the most pockmarked face
will have a pretty hole or two
if you just look carefully enough.

So do not simply criticize
our fellow countrymen,
beset as they are
with many troubles.
Seek out their strong points;
urge them on.
Is there any other way
for development and growth
to occur?"
The shadow of Inch'on somehow hovers near
this statement of policy
for the Tonga Daily newspaper.

With Dr. Syngman Rhee

From summer to winter of 1947,
somehow or other I became a close friend
of the elderly Syngman Rhee,
just back from America.
Once or twice each week
we would meet, the father of our country
and I, the poet prodigy.
He would tell stories of things that had happened,
and I would carefully write it all down.
We might share a choice apple,
on rainy days.
As we two read the poem
he had written in Chinese
on the subject of his worrying
whether he would become president,
we were support and comfort
for one-another.

But when, based on this intimacy,
I wrote his biography,
I neglected to attach the proper honorific
to his father's name.
The gentleman-by-then-turned-president
imposed a total ban
on the book's distribution.
For years after, this turn of events
left me saddened,

and for the longest time, no matter
how I tried, I could not understand.

Not, that is, until I passed
my sixtieth and sixty-first birthdays,
and experienced for myself
the meaning of that old saying
about the elderly: "The older you grow,
the more like a child you become."

Secretary for Administration

On August 15, 1948,
the government of Korea
came back to life.
At news of an examination
for section administrative staff
I became so excited, I ran all the way
to find it.
I passed easily,
and was named First Secretary for Arts,
Ministry of Education.

Our salaries were not sufficient
for enough food,
so at lunch to avoid ill feeling
among the other section staff
who might be chewing on a piece of bread
—no lunch box—
I made do with a bit of rice cake.

Our section was put in charge
of movie censorship,
and when some director came looking
for me
and said "Why
don't we go have some lunch?"
I couldn't say no.
We went to a place
with a name like *chihwajane*

where there seemed to be a number
of women.
When the worthy First Secretary
was seated on a thick cushion
the women would all rush in
to pamper and cosset me, saying
"Oh, your Lordship Mr. Secretary,
Oh your Directorship,
please take plenty of everything."
They even went so far
as to pick out the best morsels
with their chopsticks and put them
into my mouth.
Since a first secretary
was the same level as a county chief,
if this were all back
in Yi Dynasty days,
I very well might have been
such a thing as a lord.

However that might have been,
some informer must have passed along the word,
for on the very next day that I went,
the honored and honorable gentlemen of the press
followed close behind.
I became so alarmed
I couldn't have managed that method
of fast-breaking if I had wanted.
There was nothing to do but wait
for the rich food that came by American relief

once in a while,
like rice cakes in a dream.

Wolt'an said to me, "My Lord
of the Proper Name, how
exceedingly well you appear."
From time to time he would tease me
like that.
Inside there was something wrong.
I was passing blood most of the time,
so after eleven months
of all this, I gave it up.

Autumn, 1949
— At the "Flower" Tea Room

For poems the pay was a dollar
and a half. Prose
was even cheaper.
We were waiting, all of us
literary people,
for payment,
at the edge of autumn,
1949,
sitting there idly waiting
in the "Flower" tea room.

I was fated to have no alternative
to joining that number of specimens
solid as *Ansŏng* brass,
strangely suspended there.
I was president of the poetry division
of the Korean Writers Association,
established for the first time
in our country,
and while I knew I must conduct myself
with the proper sense of dignity,
I would sit there hoping that someone
else would pay the bill
for my tea.

Liberation had come to us
through another's strength;
and in this land gone mad,
split in two pieces quite unable
to work in unison,
freedom was no better
than horseshoes on a dog!
Talk of Self-Determination
was just mumbling in our sleep.

With our stomachs always hungry near sundown
for having made lunch and dinner both
out of breakfast,
dazed,
sitting there in our band
of the bewildered,
vacantly, vacantly, always
just vacantly we sat there
for our sorrowful eternity,
there in the "Flower" tea room.
There, in the "Flower" tea room!

Morning Dive in the
Han River
— June 28, 1950 —

"Why,
would those rich
little American bastards
come over and fight us?
They're not coming! They won't come!
So don't you worry, just get on with it!
Crush the South!
Generalissimo Stalin will stand by us,
so Attack! Attack!"

At that command
of Kim Il Sung the chieftain,
our land was devastated.
Farmers fleeing with their oxen
filled South Gate Boulevard
in Seoul.
His Excellency, President
Syngman Rhee
crossed the Han River foot bridge,
and in the middle of the night
ran off to the south with his company,
each and every one.
Fearing others might cross it somehow,
they blew the bridge at three
in the morning.

So it happened that on the morning
of June 28, 1950,
Cho Chihun, Yi Hanjik and I
were up on the cliffs,
up by Wŏnhyoro,
looking out at the boats
off shore.
Throwing our lives ahead, we just
plunged like bugs into the water.

Ho-Whee! Whatever else you may say,
the most useful thing at a time like that
is a bit of that so-called courage.

We managed, barely, to board
one of those so-called boats,
and joined forces with all those
running away to the south.
That's how it went.
Our dive that morning
was truly the *harmony* of harmonies.

Potassium Cyanide Left

Early August, 1950;
the communist invaders were pushing
close to an area thirty *li* north of Taegu.
Masan had fallen, and in the battle,
Ch'ae Pyŏngdŏk, Armed Forces Chief of Staff.
Our little heap of fellows
had come to resemble rotted grain
stuffed in sacks.
Preparing for the very worst,
we went and asked the chief of press
in Troop Information
to give our Writers Group in Service to the Army
some poison too.
"Sorry, but the civilians have all
bought the last of the less
painful drugs.
All I have left is bitter
potassium cyanide.
I managed to have some
set aside. Here—
Divide it up among you."
The hell with them!
If we did get chased as far down as Pusan,
then up on some hill with the sea in full view
we would mix up the cyanide with *soju*
and drink it down, chanting *Arirang*
and the National Anthem,
so even the writers group in service to the Army
could stiffen and die in some style.

Life No Better Than Death

The cruel, fratricidal war,
the corpses of all those who met untimely death
littering the ground, soaked in blood,
was not for poets a reality to be confronted.
In the sky a vast hole opens
from which things that do not exist in reality
come forth, filling the sight.
Then the poet is struck dumb.
Whether the army under MacArthur
pushed on to the Yalu or not;
whether or not he was relieved of command
in turn by Truman,
while in the interval Kim Il Sung summoned
Mao's communist army and again
descended upon the south,
blowing a bugle:
to ignore these, and to lie
down in a bed of comfortable silence,
abandoning all thought
of refuge or honor
truly constitutes an easy way
to become more and more comfortable
with those things spilling
from that hole in the sky.
For the one who turns
that way, there is no point
even in the sentence of death.
So I heard at the time
was the life and the death
of Kim Tongin.

Suicide Failure

In 1951, in Chŏnju
for the entire summer I thought
"How can I manage to kill
myself so it will seem to others
a natural death?"
I could not abide the thought
of later generations pointing me out
as the weakling suicide.

I had a mild fever
and insisted it was malaria.
I managed to obtain a bottle
of one hundred medicine tablets
and swallowed them all.
They said it was plenty
to kill five, so my death
should have been guaranteed
five times over.
Vomiting azalea-colored
blood, I kept explaining
"It wasn't suicide. I wanted
to get better more quickly;
that's why I did it."

But if the luck is gone,
even this won't work out.
The poet Yi Ch'ŏlgyun
happened at just the right moment

to find me.
He brought a most capable doctor
from the nearby hospital,
who saw to a most thorough purging.

For the twenty years or so
since then, with that one bit
of falsehood, "To get better more quickly,"
I kept my suicidal intent, at least,
well hidden; unspoken.
For the truth of it was
not body but my soul
I did want to put more quickly
to rest.

An Exercise in Harmony

Second semester, 1952,
I became a thirty measures of barley
per month associate professor
at Mr. Pak Ch'olung's
Korea University in Kwangju.
Taking a portion of that barley
to market and selling it,
I barely managed to buy my son's
school supplies.

Early one summer morning
as I was walking upstream
along the bank of the Kwangju River,
a cloud in the sky just at that moment
seemed so beautiful, all
green pea, silver, lilac and paulownia flower
colors I fell in love with on the spot.
And then the sun rising over Mudŭng Mountain
like a million babies laughing;
I was so glad, so grateful
I did not know what to do with myself.

I came back home and shouted it.
I went off to Taehung Temple at Haenam,
scraped off all my hair with a knife
and fasted for fifteen days.

As I emerged from my fast,
legs trembling, and saw the lilac bush
blooming beside the grave marker
of Yun Sŏndo, the poet known as
Lone Mountain, I thought
Yes! I am not what I was,
and my appetite
                    for life
                              is back!

In Praise of *Makkŏlli*

At Sŏrabŏl College for the Arts,
the Shanty on South Mountain

With all the buildings in Seoul of any note
destroyed in the War,
we put together a shack up on Namsan
for our Sŏrabŏl College of the Arts,
and gave most of our lectures on credit.
With our hungry stomachs, we teachers
climbed our way panting to the foot
of the mountain, where the staff
of the education affairs section
would ready the *makkŏlli* in a bucket.
"Please have a few bowls before your lecture."
— With such kindness they looked after us.
Thus I came to realize suddenly, once again,
how *makkŏlli* is indeed
one of the best things there is.

Friends of the Myŏngch'ŏnok
in Myŏngdong

In ruined Seoul from winter of '53
to spring of 1960,
when the sun began to go down
into the hazy dusk, a few friends
of no resources
more than the coins in their pockets
— Kim Tongni, Hwang Sunwŏn, Chŏng Hanmo,
and I— would gather at the Myŏngch'ŏn,
the rice-soup house in Myŏngdong.
Makkŏlli, radish leaf stew,
a dish of green-pea jelly,
and one of raw oysters:
those foods we all enjoyed,
far too much for any one of us to bear,
were brought in all together
as we raked up every last coin in our pockets,
set up the Soup Stock and Wine Company
and ate at last.
Accountant for our joint-venture firm
of scraped-together capital
was the ever-tight Kim Tongni,
who carried out his duties
without a slip.

And we always came to the chorus
"In this world of wind-blown dust,
Oh whatever am I to do?
Whatever am I to do?
We sang it out for six or seven years,
so if the lengths were laid out end to end,
they would encircle this narrow
peninsula country several thousand times
with still some bit of it left over.

Soup Stock and Wine Company:
The original, *chusik*, constitutes a pun
meaning *food-and-wine* as well as shares
of stock.

Free Literature Prize from the Asia Foundation of America

The first literary prize in my life,
I learned that too was something the Americans
were going to give me.
For my formal attire, my wife
stayed up late at night sewing a Korean coat
of black-dyed cotton.
Her fingernails became stained by that dye.

As a most dignified American lady
prepared to make the presentation,
in my confusion I completely botched
my response in English.
"Thank you. My name is Sŏ Chŏngju"
became "Sank you. I aim Sŏ Chŏngju."

Yet with the prize money I bought
a gold ring for my wife, my mother,
and my mother-in-law,
the first time in their lives
such a thing had been seen of me.
I began to be noticed, as if
all wonders in this life
can be seen with the eyes opened wide
in amazement. I was most indebted,
this once, for the American people's favor.

Second Fast

So is there anything
at all
wonderful to do?
I stayed in
fasting for another fifteen days.
Going hungry
comes to seem like the daily meal
when you develop
a taste for it.
And again I had my anxious
head scraped clean,
thought of John the Baptist
in the wilderness.
"St. John
put on a shirt
of camel's hair,
and to eat, took
locusts and honey."
So I
rested,
assuming
the form
John the Baptist might have taken,
in all that I have read
the most heroic
by far.
And when I

rose again,
I took locusts
and roasted them
and Hah! Ha-ha!
I *did* like them!

Fainting Spell

Around the end of first semester
1956
I was a part-time lecturer
at Tongguk University
and in the middle of a lecture,
"Studies on Silla,"
dressed in my white coat
of Hansan ramie-cloth
I grew suddenly faint
from hunger.
Now as I think back,
at least I kept my wits.
"Dostoevsky in an epileptic seizure
experienced a strange ecstasy,
did he not? While I have not attained
that state, I must, at least, bear up
like the brave *hwarang* knights."

And so I did not tumble flat,
but grasped the lectern's edge
and stood, bowed over,
to that extent indeed
remaining the aesthetician.

At Sŏrabŏl in Miari

There being assembled
those young men who
in all the Republic
counted their experiences the most bitter
seen by young eyes
in the horrors of the war,
the young poet-aspirants
would have choked with sorrow
at the thought they might have been
second to any in the world.
And there in 1958
in the lecture hall at Sŏrabŏl University
I was shouting out "Write only
the most breathtaking, breathtaking poems!"
quite in accordance
with the temper of that crowd.
When I hurried off to the cheap restaurant
run by the Chinese
and drank *ppaegal*
mixed with "Fan" brand digestive tonic,
those student types would follow along
and say "Let's have a drink together."
If I said "All right, but just one or two
and then off with you,"
they never listened.
"Let's go out back,
to the Good Sound Market,

and rinse out the *ppaegal*
with a round of *makkŏlli.*"

They would drag me off to some shack
down the alley where we sang
Not a flower stays red for ten days,
and the moon when it's full starts to wane.
So just play. While you are young
if you don't play, what else will you do?

We pounded on the table as we sang,
bellowing the verse at the tops of our voices.
Once a public cemetery, that place
was sold not long ago and became
the Good Sound Market.
When it rained, when it rained, I too
would bellow away at the top of my voice.

Doubts at a Doubtless Age

Pulled an aching tooth,
longing for the hills
I went up by XX Mountain
to seek out a field of hemp.
Not the field of the ginseng
of longevity,
but the kind that is used
for yellow hemp cloth,
what the Hemp-Clothed Prince wore
as he crossed over Cut-Hair Pass
on his way to become a monk.

I went up where the May bugs,
blue as a deep waterfall pool,
went swarming up *wing, wing, wing,*
and followed after a voice I could hear
of some girls high school graduate
reciting a poem.
As it hovered by my ear,
I knew it was a poem
I had written,
and I looked at her
more attentively, for she seemed
the loveliest thing in the world.
Afterward, at this age
of no doubts, I wandered
through two winters, searching
like the mute who ate the honey.

Neither to the girl
nor to anyone else beneath the heavens
did I tell a word
of this realization.

> *Doubtless Age*: One is supposed
> to have no more doubts past forty.

April 19, 1960

"A person could be killed
for anything at all.
You don't know what,
so be especially careful today."
I did not like
any of my premonitions,
the morning of April 19,
1960, and earnestly
admonished my son
Sunghae as he started
on his way to school.
It was as I feared.
The vanguard of the student demonstrations
ran far ahead, up toward Kyŏngmudae,
the president's residence,
and was cut down, they said,
by a sudden volley.
In all the turmoil,
my son remembered
my admonition and came back safe
through the alleys of T'ongwi-dong.
More than the right or wrong of it,
more than anything else
in this single thing
I was truly blessed.

April Revolution   2

Master A and Master C,
two young poet students
at K High School
were visiting my home
in the time just before
the April Revolution.
A few days after the nineteenth,
Master C appeared alone one day
and told me
the following:

"They were saying
things had gone crazy
down by City Hall,
and the two of us,
A and I,
went down to see.
But when the shooting started
Bang and Bang in all directions
we grabbed hands
the two of us
and ran like mad.
But A was hit
by a bullet
and died and
I was left
all alone
alive."

Disaster

A day or two, or perhaps more, following the May 16 coup d'etat by Major Park Chung Hee, I was forced to go with a certain policeman. Without even the faintest idea of the reason, I was taken away and put into prison. I was terribly nervous, and lay awake until late at night with my eyes wide open, while outside the cell the guards were whispering "This one is as good as dead already."

I was truly out of luck— I could not help but think it. I heard from those going in and out of the interrogation room such things as "Yi Chongdae— We have him here. The leader of those gangs in the Liberal party days. And Cho Yongsu, the publisher of the Nationalist Daily. You know; the leader of the radicals..."

I felt my flesh creep at these words. Some time before being brought in, I received a postcard from someone who introduced himself as a certain Dr. Cho—che, president of a group of professors. He wrote "...and we appoint you a member of the organization."

I paid little attention to it, neglecting even to send back notice that I declined. But this, I now had to believe, was the radical group I had heard mentioned. I did not know where the office was located, and I hadn't applied for membership, certainly. I had never even once taken part in any of their meetings, so I had no idea at all whether it was an organization that warranted arrest or not, but with the matter now coming to such a pass, this trap I had somehow fallen into was too much to endure.

The temporary chief of prison, some middle or upper level official, summoned me. Holding in front of my eyes a banner for Kim Il Sung's Democratic People's Republic, he said "You know exactly what this is, don't you! Your students were carrying this thing in a demonstration!" I was dumbstruck. It would have been quite useless for me to try to explain at that point my own personal anti-communist activities during the period since Liberation.

"Just until we have that Cho —che fellow and all his cohorts rounded up..." I was put back in the cell to wait. One day passed; then two, five, ten, fifteen... The weight of an uncertain but growing sense of resignation increased as I was drawn through this sequence of events, I began to realize it was indeed the kind of situation one might die in. At that, I could do no more than laugh a fool's laugh.

It was indeed unfortunate for Professor Cho and his real adherents, but after some fifteen days had passed, I was called again by the chief of prison, who this time held out a nice bowl of beef and rice soup. With an awkward smile, he said "Please have this, and then you are free to go. Director Cho has been captured, and we now know everything. Ha ha ha. Now that this is over, I can tell you... You know Professor Ch'oe —hwan at Seoul National University, don't you. Well, he is my maternal uncle."

That's what he said. I did and I didn't know this Ch'oe.

He was a professor at Seoul National, while I was at Tongguk. The two of us were both quite sufficiently poor to have hired out as day-labor lecturers at such places as the University for Korean Studies. When we happened to ride the same taxi-van, we knew one another only well enough to quarrel over the fare, saying "Here, let me get it this time."

Hah! If one does want to live with a foot in this world, take heed of this. Take heed!

Note: Yi Chongdae and Cho Yongsu were later executed.

Solution for a
Middle-Aged Passion

To ease the middle-aged gentleman's passion
above all else
on a date the other should be
a clear-eyed lady monk
or nun.
And further:
if the first words of introduction were
"How then might one turn
this deep red to pink,"
or something like it,
that would do very well.
And then next, or next
after next: "Does
this pink seem suitable? Like the color
of the bubbling brook waters
make it just like That!
Refreshingly right."

                              ...and
so on, and so forth...
That will do it,
don't you think?

Quote: Could I Commit an Act that Heaven would Despise?

Suppose an unmarried, mature
woman
advocate of free love
were to appear in the second
half of your fortieth year
and say "I have come to love you;
I love you constantly,
but you didn't know."
Assuming you are
already the head of a household
with wife and children:
what would be the proper thing
to do in such a situation?

Are we then to play
with one-another, thinking
"Good for you is good for me"?
Or not, saying "Endure
it, bear and suffer
it"?

Such a test
did befall me, just once
and truly
as if by accident, later
in my fortieth year.

Best to keep
the result a secret;
for if "Good for you is
good for me," stones
and insults follow,
whereas
had I advised her
simply to endure,
"Damn! You! Playing
so innocent,
so aloof...!"
Suspended in disbelief.

As Confucius said,
with regard to such occasions
Ask, "Could I then commit an act
that heaven would despise?"

Putting that thought into practice,
I shall remain silent.

Counting Longevity by
a Child Late in Life

For those wishing to enjoy a long life
well past the age of seventy,
the best way is to have a child
after passing the age of forty.
To borrow another's
womb is far more complicated
than to proceed with your wife's
whom you wed in poverty,
so proceed with her.

These days, caught in the midst
of the "Have Just Two" movement,
avoid anything of that nature
in the twenties and thirties.
Take what heaven leaves you
and have the child late.

No matter how cold,
no matter how impatient a person may be,
he will know the way
to cherish his own child,
and for the child's sake
how to care for himself.
Taking a doctorate in this caring,
how long would it take, all together?

Six years before school, and six of primary;
six of middle and high school,
and four for the university.
Then three years of the military,
and five of graduate school,
which makes how much, all told?
Six
six
six
four
three
five:
          How many years is that?
If you manage to live as long as that sum,
won't your longevity be assured?

Abraham, long, long ago,
when he started a child
in the womb of his elderly wife,
did so for that very reason,
no doubt.

Five Years on the Seoul-Ch'unch'ŏn Line

From around springtime, March of 1963
until the first grains of snow time
in the winter of '68,
there were so many, many distractions
on the line from Seoul down to Ch'unch'ŏn,
and I became one with them
as I strolled around the train.
The lecture fee once a week
from XX Womens College
could hardly be called satisfactory,
so I suppose it was inevitable
I passed the time letting my eyes wander
this way and that:
at arrowroot blossoms in thickets that twined
over potato-shaped rocks,
the potato-wine *makkŏlli* squeezed out beneath them,
the mad flurry of bird songs
that erupted after drinking,
and the whores from the sausage-stew place
who insinuated themselves
into the quiet moments.

And in midsummer, just at dusk
we entered the valley of Kangch'on Village,
passing through as if sinking

into a river.
At that moment, I felt
the mountain cuckoo's cry
sink into my bones,
as if from one thing
at least
my attention should not wander.

House of the Apricot Tree

There is no way at all to tell how many hundreds of years old the spirits are now of those who lived and died and planted the old apricot tree that still bloomed every year at the House of the Apricot Tree in Kongdŏk-dong. In that quarter of a century from 1945 to 1970 while my family lived there, I was never the real master of the house. No, it was that old lady, looking nicely aged, by day or night—that one, the flowering apricot tree.

Even the Chinese restaurant that Mr. Ko and his family had run for generations in the village, when they were sending a note asking for payment of my bill would address it to "The Master of the House of the Apricot Tree" rather than by name, to Sŏ Chŏngju. The fame of that old tree was known throughout the whole village.

In the season when the apricot tree was blooming, we would all sit down to share a big pot of noodles, the most sumptuous meal our poor family could afford, ordered on credit from Mr. Ko's. Our youngest, just a year old, would inch his way closer and closer to the noodles, saying "Me some. I want some." If you think about it for a while, this too was thanks to the long established credit of the old apricot tree's name.

In summer when all the flowers and fruit were gone from the tree, the quiet rustling of the leaves made of our bare yard a rural millet field, coolly rustling in our village, *sagak,*

sagak, sagak... And from listening to that constant whispering, we came to name the house *Hear Millet Hall*—That too,of course, intended to please the spirit of the old apricot tree.

Some time later, when the poet Song Yŏngt'aek approached me and asked me to give him that name, I could not refuse. I simply surrendered it, in matters of this kind, at least, not given—even I—to stinginess.

My Drinking Friend, Pak Kiwŏn

Pak Kiwŏn, also known as Yach'ŏng: I liked his style as he sat there never moving, like a stuffed crane. No matter how many kettles of wine he might put away, it never seemed to make much difference. I enjoyed the way just a bit of a laugh would emerge from his throat in its four-syllable, slightly counterfeit *Ha-ha-ha-ha.* And I liked the way he maintained that stiff posture of his, waiting for no one in particular in places like the Applause and the Elephant tearooms between eleven in the morning and eleven at night, in Myŏngdong. Whether it had been one year or two, five years or ten, and regardless of the price of *soju* or *makkŏlli,* he would always be sitting there in a way that I liked. He was five years or so older, but had become known somewhat later in the literary world. With those factors just cancelling each other out, we called each other by the plain "Hey you."

One year, at dusk on an autumn day that would bring tears to a young calf, I was trying to locate him again after a longish interval. As I poked in at the Elephant tearoom I heard "Hey you, Midang! Wouldn't you like to go meet Shin Ilsŏn, the one from the movie *Arirang?*" Of course I did. As a seventh grader, I had been enchanted when I first saw her, and now the thought of going to meet her, the actress Shin Ilsŏn, the one who had played the hero's sweetheart in the movie *Arirang...*

Down some back alley in Sorin-dong, next to Ta-dong, we went and found Shin Ilsŏn's wine house. I looked at her from every side, from every direction. The lady was already nearly sixty, with many silky wrinkles, but the sad beauty of her expressive eyes seemed the same now as it was on the screen.

"Go ahead now, just touch the back of her hand." Yach'ŏng said this with great conviction, like a gang boss speaking to an especially favored henchman. As if unable to resist his suggestion, I went ahead and did as he said. It was not as it might not have been; that is to say, it seemed as if it were quite right, all right.

Story of Ulsan Rock

There is a story that goes as follows. When God created the Diamond Mountains, he said "Let all those rocks that feel proud of themselves gather here," at which one great lump that had been living in Kyŏngsang Province, in Ulsan, confident it was the greatest rock in all the land, flew up and started for the Diamond Mountains, in Kangwŏn Province. After flying for a while, it looked around and saw the skies were crowded dark with all manner of strange stones and rocks struggling to get ahead. Thinking "What! In all my grandness, am I to join with that miscellaneous lot?" the great stone turned in midcourse and settled down on the rim of Sŏrak Mountain.

During summer vacation in 1967 I took my youngest son, then in fourth grade, off to Sŏrak Mountain to have a look at Ulsan Rock. Though I did not go so far as to say to the child "You do the same," the chance to tell him the legend of the rock was a way to hint at the lessons of my own long experience.

Drinking *Kimch'i* Juice

Sometime in 1968; I was hard pressed for money. Hoping for
a prize—it was two million *wŏn*—I took a chance with my
collection *Winter Sky*, submitting it for the XX Literary
Prize. I filled out the application form, stamped it with my
seal and signed my name, then sent it in. This was the first
time in my life that I had filled out an application for a
prize.

Now there is a common saying about drinking *kimch'i* juice
before the host has given any sign that he will bring out the
rice cakes. After sending in the application and spending
several months just swallowing my own saliva, as in the
saying, something like the lines that follow below just came
to me, quite unbidden:

If the child, hungry for fifteen days,
turns his face toward the mountain and laughs,
the child hungry for fifteen days more
turns his face toward two mountains
and laughs...

Fortune did not favor me, notwithstanding, but turned instead
toward Mr. Pak Mogwŏl. It all brought me to a real feeling,
once again, for the taste of that *kimch'i* juice in the old
saying.

Examining a Woman's Fingernails

Days when the sun is blinding bright
when all things turn unendurably transparent
like a bear kept behind the glass window
trying to escape the sightseers peering in
escaping, escaped, raise the wine glass,

for such day's are the woman's.
When the unresolved quarrel cannot be abided,
rather than into her clear eyes
look into her ten fingernails, translucent, instead.

The fingernails, like a drawn curtain
are snug, not clear at all,
and as the tiny half moons are there rising,
for a man of fifty who likes his drink,
this will be the proper limit.

As Calamity Begets
Good Fortune, Again

My next door neighbor, formerly a policeman during the
Japanese period, had a decent enough smile in his eyes and
teeth, but he kept after me so persistently to get him a
position somewhere, I asked a certain director of a certain
office, someone who simply was not in a position to ignore
me, and arranged it. Ten years after, with a fairly
comfortable life, this way and that, spent raising children
and feeding his children on a decent salary, he seemed to
have forgotten all about it. He sent for the husband of his
niece, or something like that—not a terribly bright young
fellow—and set him up as a blacksmith, unlicensed, out in
the yard. Day in and day out, *Ttuk-ddak, ttuk-ddak, ssŭrŭrŭ-
ssŭrŭrŭ, k'wang, k'wang, k'wang, k'wang,* the horrendous noise
of metal pounding on metal was rammed into my two ears,
even there in my study for writing poems. There was no
help for it. We packed up and bought a tiny lot in a field
full of thorns, over in Sadang-dong, over at the foot of
Kwanak Mountain. There we started to build our gourd-sized
house... A new house, built up on the hillside in Sadang-dong,
that weird height where the ghosts of the lowest of the low,
the temple apprentices, seemed even after death to be crying
out "Cannot live here, will not live here." In that sloppy field
of tall mugwort, one could live without a wife, but not
without a pair of high rubber boots...

From the fall of '69 until winter had gone, my wife and I

took turns in keeping watch over our construction site, not even aware of it when our toes got frozen. We asked them to please build it solidly, and tried our best to keep the workers happy with such suggestions as "Foreman Pak, won't you have a bit of these pork ribs?" and "Foreman Kim, please have a bit of this ox-head stew. Have some beer, and a shot of *soju* for a chaser."

So at last for the first time in my life I came into possession of a newly-built home. There may well be nothing much to that phrase about how calamity begets good fortune, but this is just the way it happens, when it does.

> *Sadang-dong*: During the Yi Dynasty, this part of Seoul was evidently a favorite dwelling-place for the *Sadang*, a lower class group that included apprentices and entertainers at the Buddhist temples.

The Power of Sadang-dong and Pongch'ŏn-dong

Throughout Seoul as the inhabitable places were condemned—
"Too filthy to live in!"—the people who had been chased out
gathered in the end to put up their shacks all clustered
together side by side in Sadang-dong and Pongch'ŏn-dong.
When it rained, the whole place was nothing better than a
field of mud, a place where they said it was better to live
with a pair of rubber boots than a wife. On rainy days on
my way to lecture at Tongguk University or some other
place, it took me twenty-five minutes in my rubber boots
to make it to the bus stop for Number 86. At a little hole-in-
the-wall shop, I would take off my boots and leave them, then
put on my leather shoes and climb onto the bus.

One day as I glanced around inside, I noticed that for some
reason one seat remained empty. I made my way over to
it and sat down, only to discover that it was the very spot
toward which with unerring aim the leaking roof directed
a steady stream of large drops. I was already so worn out, I just
went on sitting there, getting wetter and wetter. I didn't
care how wet.

As we stopped at the main stop on the Sadang-dong route, a
married pair of about forty, who looked as if they had been
making their eyes bloodshot since morning, pushed their way
on. They were carrying the most miserable looking collection
of packages in their hands, perched on their heads, clutched

to their chests. They were both sweating furiously. The one who seemed to be the male of the two looked like some refugee general just escaping from the swords of a thousand and the hooves of ten thousand. He laughed with a very strange *kkŭk-kkŭk-kkŭk-kkŭk* and called out to no one, "Well, shall I impose here? Shall I be an imposition over there?" One filthy heap of packages, he plopped down into the lap of a junior high school girl, and into the lap of some child of primary school age, he snuck the others.

The Taiwanese Poet Chung
Ting-wen Visits

Chung Ting-wen of Free China came to Seoul for the International Pen Club meeting with the writer Lin Yu-tang. Using the occasion of his visit, and with Mr. Ho Se'uk, one of our young poets, acting as interpreter, he paid a call at my home, there in the muddy fields below Kwanak Mountain.

After sitting and drinking a bit too much, making our way back to the Namsŏng-dong bus terminal, we happened to pass the Chinese cemetery. Exclaiming "Yah, this certainly looks familiar!" Chung Ting-wen dashed in among the graves, stopped at a certain spot, and opening his fly, proceeded to water the ground with considerable gusto. He called over, in the middle of it all, "Hey, this is the first comfortable piss I've had since I left Taiwan!"

I too was moved by this occasion, and in my boyish mood I raised my voice, praying for the repose of those Chinese dead, calling out "Namu samanda, Oh merciful Buddha, hear these words of comfort and solace for the soul in all directions."

Queen Sŏndŏk's Stone

On a certain day in a certain year—I am not certain when. Some day, one day the poet Im Songjo—it was during the time he spent as a monk at Haeinsa—visited the tomb of Queen Sŏndŏk, in Kyŏngju. "Just something to pick up," he thought, and carried back to my home, my Mountain Room there below Kwanak Mountain, a pink stone roughly the size of the *Kkokdu-kaksi* puppet. The hollow of the stone was covered with a lovely, hair-like green lichen, as if it might have been Queen Sŏndŏk's. I set the stone carefully in a spot that appealed to my eye, and every morning and evening I would water the lichen. I became quite attached to it.

The stories—that because of the Queen, Chigwi the Madman suffered his one-sided love; and that when she heard of it, the Queen placed her golden bracelets on the chest of the fellow as he lay in sleep one day; or that the Queen had made arrangements ahead of time for a proper place in heaven to live in after he had died; or even that one can tell how fragrant the peony will be simply by looking at the seed: such notions were most beguiling to me. As I considered how that stone had come to me following the thread of some predetermined connection, it became a most quiet and mysterious demonstration of beauty's truth.

Chicken Instead of Pheasant

In 1938 when my wife was seventeen and I was twenty-two, she came to my family home in marriage, bringing as a present from her parents a most extraordinarily handsome set of rosewood chests. Six years later, in the midst of the most painful deprivation near the end of the Japanese occupation in 1944, because our stomachs were empty, I decided we had to sell the wardrobe set. Though she said nothing about it, her mouth trembled and her eyes filled with tears.

Twenty-eight years went by without my being able to buy her a replacement, until in 1972 when to ease my guilty conscience, I took five-hundred thousand of the two million *wŏn* I received when my "Collected Works" was published, and bought a T'ong-yong-style, inlaid pearl set of clothing chests that she had long desired. But instead of the lively smile she had worn when she brought the rosewood chests, her smile was faint and expressionless. My own smile, as I looked at her and remembered—my own became dispirited too.

Forsythia Ghost in my Garden

One day in early spring as I happened by a little shop for garden trees in Sadang-dong, an old forsythia tree caught my eye. It was shaped like an umbrella held up above a stem stout as a warrior's wrist. I bought it at the price they asked, ten thousand *wŏn*, and had it sent to my home to be planted there. The shop man must have been pleased to get that price, for without my even asking him he told me the story of the tree with the same kind of relish that might have followed a good drink or two. The story he told went as follows.

Well, if you live long enough, there are bound to be some unusual things. There certainly will be. I was up in Kwach'ŏn Village, a little place up in the hills. I was just poking around from house to house calling out my "Sell your trees! Sell your flower trees!" when an old woman poked out of her gate and said "Come this way." I followed along to see. The shrub wasn't much; it was this very tree, in fact, this forsythia right here. "This is the tree my departed husband took care of. He pruned it for many decades. Since he died and left me, I feel sad just looking at it. I won't ask a price for it; only, dig it up quickly now and take it along with you." That's what she told me. Like I say, you see some strange things, if you live long enough. You see every kind of thing."

So it is that the ghost of this forsythia tree has left his old wife all alone and come to live in a corner of the garden by our house. His discomfort knows some relief, for it does seem apparent that in this business, the container for this ghost of the forsythia tree has been moved as well.

David McCann, Translator of
my Poems, and the Town of Andong

It was in 1974, summertime, when an American who seemed to be about thirty years old came out to my house by Kwanak Mountain. When he introduced himself as someone who believed the most important thing he could do was to translate my poems, I asked him why, with all the countries in this world, he happened to choose Korean poetry.

"Well," he said, "I graduated from Harvard College, in the United States, and entered the Peace Corps. I hoped to go to Korea, and eventually was assigned as an English teacher at the Agriculture and Forestry high School in Andong, Kyŏngsang Province."

McCann had replied with reasonable fluency in our language, smiling as he did. He went on: "To speak frankly, I still didn't know, then, just what there was that could be called real literature in Korean, so I asked one of the teachers at the high school about it. Well, that teacher just blew up at me. 'Is *that* all you think of our country? Why, isn't there any good literature in Korea? Is that what you think? No more talking about it. I'll teach you, starting with the *sijo*. I want you to learn one of them every day.' For the three years I stayed at the school, I worked hard at studying Korean literature, and have come to apprehend the extent to which Korea is indeed a country with good poetry."

After his three years in Andong, he went back to his alma mater and completed his M.A. in two years, then returned to Korea to conduct the research for his dissertation. At the time of his visit, he was auditing courses in Korean literature at Korea Univeristy.

Yet—"Andong"? As I said the name over to myself, I couldn't help but smile. The reason was that just a year before McCann's story, an incident took place in the market at Andong. Whenever I think of that place called Andong and what happened to me there, I cannot help breaking into a big grin. The story is as follows.

I had gone down to Andong to conduct the wedding of the young poet Kim Wŏn'gil. On the way there, I stopped at the Andong market, thinking I might be able to find a good straw mat, the kind to spread out in the summer for a place to sit down and have some home-made noodles. I was shopping around in the market, when by luck I spotted just the mat, spread out in a corner of one shop. The mat was big enough for ten to sit down and have their noodles, and right in the middle of it sat an old grandfather, owner of the shop, wearing in a most gentlemanly way one of the old-fashioned horsehair hats.

"What does that one go for, Grandfather?" I asked.

"Well, let's see now," he replied. "For fourteen days I've been doing nothing much but weave this mat. I won't charge you for the straw that's gone into it. If you figure it at one hundred *wŏn* a day, that would come out to fourteen-hundred, wouldn't it?"

The memory of how he said that is what comes back to me. It's the way he insisted, exactly fourteen-hundred *wŏn*. Not a thousand five hundred; not two thousand either. That is what stays with me.

Hwan'gap: Full Cycle Sixty Years   1

Since I was born in the Year of the Rabbit, I should have just lived comfortably eating grasses and plants, passing little rabbit turds, and once as an especially stupid turtle carried me on his back over the sea and implored me to give him my liver, answer "Liver have I none. Not now, anyway. I carry that sort of thing around with me only at night, you see. Do you think I would have it on me during the day? I take it out during the day and spread it on a rock to dry in the sun." But no, my father's servant's rickety memory and the county registration clerk's quirky rules of thumb combined for some reason to advance my age by one year, to the Year of the Tiger, so by the rule of how things are in the world, I had to conduct myself as a tiger would.

By that rule, my *hwan'gap* would have been celebrated in the Year of the Tiger, which my dear wife found too disconcerting. Observing it the following year, the Year of Rabbit, she went and bought a young pine tree, as Korean tradition prescribes. It was a rather short baby of a pine which she planted in the garden just outside my room. The age of this little pine must have been just about the double-eight of youthful bloom, representation of her earnest wish that I might live life to the very fullest, this time, and younger by that amount.

> *Note*: The story of the rabbit and the turtle is a favorite folk story.

Hwan'gap   2

At the time of the opening
of an exhibit of illustrated poems
commemorating my sixtieth
birthday, on Cheju Island
as huge flakes of snow were falling
Christmas Eve, the young girl
of nineteen whose tears stained

the collar of my Korean jacket
as she sat beside me
cannot be forgotten.
A graduate of some girls high school
in Chinju, working
at the wine house we happened upon,
she had recited my poem
"Beside a Chrysanthemum"
there by our table, and learned
I was the author...

The vision of that girl
who came to my side
and wept
is something I shall
never forget.

Off on a Trip Round the World

"One must appreciate the many attractions
of this life! I'll put together a collection
of poems, a travel diary,
sell it and see about living
on a hundred million *wŏn*."
With such grand ambitions,
the fellow from Chŏlla, well past
his fiftieth and sixtieth birthdays,
set forth on his wanderer's path round the world.
To Mexico, passing Canada and the States in one breath.
Cuernavaca, twenty-five hundred meters
above sea level. Hundreds of millions
of blossoms, blood red bouganvilleas
blooming like the maiden's liver
in the air one-hundred percent pure,
and in their midst, I was sitting
with my heart quite overwhelmed.
An elf of fifteen or sixteen
said "This is really the best,"
and held out a container
of some greenish, elf's brew.
I drank it up and my insides
turned upside down.
When I added a bit too much
to drink as a chaser,
Oh Lord! At once,
everything before my eyes turned black
and I fell flat on top of the table.

Committed to the hospital, I was brought
back to life by the respirator
and other means.
Returned to Mexico City,
this time I threw up blood,
threw up blood
over and over, all the color
of bouganvilleas.
I was filled up again with blood
borrowed from the Mexican people,
and decided to suppress my cravings.
Slowly, slower, and quietly,
and yet more quietly,
I would make my way by the round-about,
Z-shaped path of the mountain spirit.

Doctor of Letters at Sixty, and my Mother

For some reason afflicted
with the fate of being late
for everything,
after thirty years'
lecturing at the university
I missed the doctorate that often comes
on the fiftieth birthday.
I came in line for it again
at sixty, but perhaps because I had passed
through some neutral sex toward
the feminine, I received
my Doctor of Letters
from Sookmyung Women's University.

As I thought "Just who
would say this is the best thing ever
to happen in life?"
I realized it was my widowed mother,
just turned ninety.
For the first time in my life
managing something in the way of proper
filial piety,
I wrapped up the doctor's cap and gown
and brought the package to my mother.
I put them on and showed her,
then had my mother wear them too.

My mother spoke to me then
with the honorific form of address,
saying "Do come here,
our honored Doctor Sŏ."
Though she had no idea
what a poet was, she knew
well enough about Ph. D.
She seemed quite thoroughly
delighted, as she said
"So it is you, our very own
Doctor Sŏ?

"Know Grandson" Orchid

The day I gave the name *Chison,*
"Know Grandson," to the orchid
my wife dug up and brought
down from grandfather's
mountain tomb,
the thought came to me
with extraordinary vividness
of Go-in, my grandson,
now studying in a far-away land.

Professor Emeritus

Having been a lecturer for a long time, at retirement from Tongguk University there are three categories of title for the retiree. The first is Professor by merit; the second, professor by courtesy of salary; the third, full-time graduate school faculty. But the full-time graduate faculty were the only ones whose salaries did not become less; the professor emeritus and the salaried professor encountered an appropriate reduction, with the emeritus cut mercilessly and the salaried professor cut to only about half that of the graduate faculty.

The wise man's middle of the road approach seemed most suitable of the three; and besides, for a poet to have had the good luck to receive even the mediocre salary enabled my wife and me to get along together with enough, just enough, to live on. Yet it did seem that when someone else heard this title of salaried professor it sounded like something less than full professor, a point that remained a shameful one to me.

When I explained this to the chancellor, saying "Shouldn't the better-sounding title of professor emeritus be given to the one who earns the better salary, no matter how small the increment?" he replied "That's fine. If you want to call yourself professor emeritus, go right ahead. In terms of salary, the salaried professor is really one grade higher, but the difference doesn't amount to much anyway." So that is how we arranged it, and I have gone on working ever since.

Principal Literary Figures Mentioned in the Poems

Chang Chunha (1918-1975)   Publisher of the monthly journal *Sasanggye, World of Thought;* died while hiking near Seoul on the thirtieth anniversary observance of his return to Korea from exile in Xian, China, shortly before Liberation.

Cho Chihun (1920-1968)   Poet and cultural historian; taught at Korea University.

Ch'oe Chŏnghŭi (Born 1912)   Novelist. Her *In'gansa, History of Humankind,* published in the journal *Sasanggye* (see under Chang Chunha) is one of her best known works.

Ch'oe Namsŏn (1890-1957)   Pioneering writer, Korean cultural historian, publisher, and author of the 1919 Proclamation of Korean Independence.

Chŏng Hanmo (Born 1923)   Poet and literary historian; professor of Korean literature at Seoul National University.

Han Yongun (1879-1944)   Poet, priest, patriot; one of the thirty-three signers of the 1919 Proclamation of Korean Independence. His collection of poems *Nimŭi ch'immuk, The Silence of Love,* remains one of the truly seminal works of twentieth century Korean literature.

Hwang Sunwŏn (Born 1915)   One of Korea's most influential novelists. Several of his works have been published in English translation, including *Namudŭl pit'ale sŏda, Trees on the Cliff*, originally published in 1960, and *Umjiginŭn Sŏng, The Moving Castle*, originally published in serial form 1968-1972.

Ishikawa Takuboku (1885-1912)   Japanese poet.

Kim Tongin (1900-1951) Novelist and short story writer; studied in Japan and graduated from Meiji University in 1917. An immensely prolific writer through the 1920's, 1930's, and 1940's. Known as a truly innovative stylist. His *Kamja, Potatoes,* has become one of the most widely anthologized examples of modern Korean literature. In failing health, he died in Seoul during the North Korean occupation of the city.

Kim Tongni (Born 1913)   One of Korea's best known and most honored novelists.

Manhae (Pen name; see Han Yongun)

Pak Chonghwa (1901-1981)   Author of numerous poems, stories, novels, and other works; president of many of Korea's literary organizations.

Pak Mogwŏl (1916-1978)   Poet; born in Kyŏngju, North Kyŏngsang Province. A superb and inspired poet of the natural world, especially in his earlier works. Many more of his poems deserve to be translated into English. (Mogwŏl was his pen name; his name was Pak Yŏngjong.)

Pyŏn Suju (1898-1961) Poet, and scholar of English literature. Graduated from college in California; translated the Proclamation of Korean Independence into English. (Suju was his pen name; his name was Pyŏn Yŏngno.)

Wolt'an (Pen name; see Pak Chonghwa.)

Yun Sŏndo (1587-1671) *Sijo* poet and scholar. Known particularly for the *sijo* sequences *Ŏbusasisa, The Fisherman's Calendar*, and *Ouga, Song of the Five Friends*.